Mental Wealth

Unlock your potential, enrich your life

MIKE PAGAN

Mental Wealth

ISBN 978-1-912300-44-0

eISBN 978-1-912300-45-7

Published in 2021 by SRA Books

© Mike Pagan 2021

Scripture quotations are taken from the Holy Bible, New Living Translation, copyright ©1996, 2004, 2015 by Tyndale House Foundation. Used by permission of Tyndale House Publishers, Carol Stream, Illinois 60188, United States. All rights reserved.

Contents

The Mastermind Team

The Mental Wealth Team Summary

The Mental Wealth Team Scorecard

Time to Get on with It!

Foreword

Alvin Law

I want to thank Mike Pagan for this book. As a Canadian Hall of Fame Professional Speaker, I've addressed the issue of mental health for decades.

I am a 'Thalidomide baby' born in 1960, and I was born without arms. So I have had 'challenges'. I didn't realise I was living Mental Wealth right from the start because of the incredible support network I experienced growing up in a small, rural community in Canada. Everyone in town 'had my back', so I could more than just survive... but truly thrive.

I'm proud to have Mike Pagan's back in supporting this excellent book that dives deep into mental health, and uses everyday language to help everyone understand that no matter how tough things may appear, we can get through it... together!

Everyone counts... Everyone!

Preface

In the latter stages of writing this book, a friend asked if I'd heard the news about Tom. I knew Tom through my son's school and rugby activities, and he attended family celebrations. I told my friend no, I hadn't heard the news about Tom – but I already knew where this was going.

Tom had committed suicide. The words hit me in the pit of my stomach, and I became totally numb.

I knew that Tom had experienced family problems after a difficult divorce. But I had no idea his situation had become so desperate.

As the numbness subsided, it struck me that his support network, of which I was an extended part, had failed. Maybe he didn't have the correct people around him asking the right questions.

People suffering from mental health issues are often experts at concealing the challenges they're facing from their nearest and dearest. Many make a big noise and are big characters on a night out, but they can often be the most fragile underneath.

Maybe if Tom had had the right support network around him, watching out for worrying signs, gently challenging him when necessary, there might have been a different outcome.

Maybe if I had reached out more often... There are a hundred maybes, and none of them will help with the grief and guilt suffered by those left behind. Nobody will ever know what might have made a difference.

It made me realise that we must challenge each other and reach out to those we haven't spoken to for a while. And if something doesn't feel, smell or seem right, then it's our responsibility as human beings, friends, lovers or even strangers to ask questions and not let it go.

This book can change lives and potentially save lives. I believed this before I heard the tragic news about Tom – and now I believe it even more passionately. And no, his real name isn't Tom. Out of respect for his family, I chose not to use it.

The kind of support network I'm talking about is what I call a mental wealth team. Because there are times when we all need backing from different people, and having the right network around us, looking out for us, can make all the difference.

This book is designed to dip in and out of, or you may choose to read it from cover to cover in one hit. Whichever way you do it, the challenge is to work on the conclusions that you come to as a result of reading the book. What actions will you take, and how will you anchor and implement the learnings?

What follows is a kick in the proverbials for your personal development and growth. Use it in the way that best suits you; if that means writing all over it, ripping out the relevant pages and pinning them on the back of the toilet door, then go for it.

It's written in plain English, with no management jargon. You will not need a thesaurus. The ideas and reminders are designed to be straight-forward and acted upon the moment you read them, or challenge you to seek help where necessary. My hope is that you will gain a sense of pride and confidence in focusing on who you need to surround yourself with in order to thrive.

My approach is often light hearted, but always has a serious message. By selecting the appropriate mental wealth team, you can gain more control over your mental health while having a direct impact on your levels of success and prosperity. In order to succeed, you'll need to build new habits and improve your questioning skills of those around you.

What Is Mental Wealth?

Mental wealth is a combination of optimum mental health and the backing of a committed support network that I refer to as a mental wealth team. A key benefit of having such a team is a sense of inner security and purpose, with added laughter, fun and enjoyment along the way. With a team assisting you in the pursuit of your true potential and wellbeing, you can positively impact your mental and physical performance.

It's important to start with the understanding that we're all on a mental health spectrum that is ever changing. Your mental health can be very positive, or it can be very harmful to you, depending on where you sit along the spectrum at any given time.

The standard definition of wealth is 'a plentiful supply of a particular desirable thing'. It could be said that you are wealthy, or lacking in wealth, at different times in your life – and the same applies to mental wealth.

Setting aside the traditional ways of building financial wealth, for me the goal of mental wealth is 'the simple life' – to be doing what I love and to love what I do, surrounded by the people I love, who love me.

Why you need a mental wealth team

A mental wealth team helps you deal with the isolation that is part of everyone's lives. We are social animals and need support and input from others; separation can cause stress and heartache, kill creativity and prevent decision-making. In many cases it is the direct cause of failure. Isolation is not something you can avoid, but it is something you can manage and control (more on this later).

By embracing the collective wisdom of a team, you'll receive so many insights that can make a positive difference. In scuba diving, you check your equipment first and then assist your buddy. You are no use to others if you are stressed and anxious.

Society dictates that being selfish is terrible; however, looking after yourself first, with the right team supporting you, means you are capable of caring for and helping others. My objective is to help you get better answers from the people around you, while providing the necessary tools to help you build the appropriate mental wealth team.

In order to be fit for purpose, you need the support of others; you cannot do it on your own. When you take shortcuts, or choose to reject help from others, expensive mistakes and self-created problems occur. With just a pinch of hindsight, you realise they were considerable errors of judgement.

A mental wealth team (and this book) consists of four key components – each one will vary in importance depending on the individual. Throughout each section, I will share tools and ideas that will pose questions about how you seek support, use your networks and strive to achieve more.

I'll be looking at:

- **self-care that nurtures your mind, body, wellbeing, nutrition and spiritual needs**

- **the right coach for the path ahead – unlocking greater potential than you can achieve on your own**

- **your team of professionals: wealth manager, legal eagle, accountant**

- **the mastermind group: peer support, empowering others to hold you accountable while you provide the same support for them in a mutually supportive ecosystem.**

Having a mental wealth team has made a massive difference to me, both personally and professionally. It reassures me that I am not alone in making decisions as a businessman, husband, father and human being. I can bounce ideas around with the team, which stops me searching for permission from another source or higher body before I make decisions.

I would never have been able to perform on stage in front of thousands of people, completed international business qualifications or become a proud father of three wonderful young adults if I didn't have the correct mindset.

I believe I have developed my talents and abilities through hard work, continuous learning and failure, commonly known as a growth mindset. This stands in opposition to a fixed mindset, which believes it's better or safer not to risk failure. Having a mental wealth team gives me the safe space to fail and the support network to rebuild.

You need to have the strength to ask for help and then act upon it. If that help is not in your current support network, then create the mental wealth team that works for you.

Who should be on your mental wealth team?

When it comes to building a mental wealth team, there is no 'one size fits all'. We are all from different backgrounds and cultures and have different beliefs. Before you can build your team, it is essential to understand where the weaknesses are in your current environment, be they people, goals or your general direction in life. With a greater understanding of these, it then becomes so much easier to figure out who will be the best fit for you.

There are so many people you could call upon to become part of your support network; the challenge is being specific about who you want to be involved and how they can help. It's not about having thousands of names in your database or on social media. This is a proactive team that is there to support you, look out for you, challenge you and be there for you in the good times and the bad.

Everybody fails, and failing becomes so much easier when you have people to talk to, to help you get back up and carry on, or to help you understand what happened so you can learn from it and improve. A mental wealth team will help you fail better and be brave enough to take risks with the knowledge that you are not alone.

A word about mental health

The topic of mental health is very much at the forefront of health and wellbeing at present, and rightly so. It is a huge hidden challenge for so many, and those suffering often wear the best disguises. I'm not a mental health practitioner or psychologist, but I am a trained mental health first-aider – a qualification I believe everyone should acquire, especially as mental health first-aiders are likely to become mandatory for organisations, in conjunction with existing first aid officers.

I started looking into performance, happiness and productivity for several reasons. I work with clients who enjoy positive mental health and those who are struggling with their mental health. Their situations range from procrastination and faffing about (doing stuff that at best keeps you busy but isn't what you should be or need to be doing) to severe depression and anxiety.

Where my own mental health is concerned, members of my family have often likened my sporting activities to a type of self-harm, because of the amount of training, dedication and sacrifice I put into them. My reaction in the past was to feel that this was harsh; I just happen to enjoy my sport, so I do a lot of it. However, there have been times when, if I'm entirely honest, some of my activities – such as the big runs, quadrathlons and swimming the English Channel – could well have been avoidance and distraction tactics.

Sometimes it feels easier to do the training and the activity rather than the work or the chores that aren't as much fun or that I just don't like doing. My discipline with regard to fitness far outweighs the discipline I apply to my business development or making phone calls. Having a mental wealth team gives me perspective and gets me back on track and away from faffing about and distractions. I know this type of self-harm has affected my performance, my bank balance and levels of success in other areas of my life.

The later chapters will share some of the techniques and tactics that I use to manage my focus and mitigate my ability to self-harm. These techniques help me maintain my mental health and keep me pure and grounded, from wellbeing to fitness, health, nutrition and diet.

How do you measure and get better at mental wealth?

Unlike financial wealth, there is no such thing as a simple calculation for your mental wealth, because everyone has a unique combination of programming, history and drivers. My aim is to help you identify the specific elements that have an impact on your mental wealth, but it's all about finding the measurement criteria that are relevant to you.

It is important to understand what you do when you're firing on all cylinders, and the things that help you, versus the things that sabotage your performance and happiness – which can go all the way back to childhood.

Too many parents condition their children by saying: 'It's got to be done the right way.' My father used to describe it as 'The Pagan Way', i.e. to comply to his standards. Unfortunately, a child doesn't have this perspective, and it can result in failures later in life. Trying to live up to other people's expectations can profoundly affect mental wealth.

When you have suitable people helping you on your journey, and you know how to ask for help, your mental wealth grows exponentially. As your team steps up to support you, the magic kicks in, success becomes easier to achieve and it becomes a lot more fun as well.

Part of my mental wealth mission is to have a lot more fun in everything that I do, whether that be work, play, family, travel, or even yodelling on the top of a mountain! Having more fun is a key ingredient of mental wealth (I talk about this in a lot more detail in the self-care section). Remember that accepting the status quo is a choice, and the status quo comes with both positive and negative baggage. Time to step up and make some decisions!

Isolation vs loneliness

Working and existing in isolation kills creativity and prevents simple decision-making. This is one of the reasons why prisons use isolation as a punishment. As humans, we need others to spark off, generate ideas and collaborate with.

I know it's not just me that has a little voice in my head that gets louder the more isolated I become, as my mind craves interaction. In 2020, millions of people across the world went into various stages of isolation in the coronavirus pandemic, delivering a serious increase in mental health issues and suicide rates.

According to the Office of National Statistics, for 2020 the figures for the UK show suicide rates to be the highest for more than 20 years, at just over 11 deaths per 100,000 people. Fortunately, we are not at the levels reached in the early 1980s, but these numbers are undoubtedly understated due to the fact that official figures only count a death as a suicide where there is clear evidence that it was intentional and a note was left.

There is so much work to be done here. The different mental outlooks between being alone and being lonely are huge. It's crucial to know which one is relevant to you at any particular time.

Picture the scene. You are sitting in a bar writing a newsletter, reading a book or catching up with the news. There may be people around you or you may be alone, but that doesn't mean you are lonely, just on your own. Solitude doesn't necessarily equal loneliness. It is often a choice. There are times when you want to be alone, in an environment without noise and distraction.

Seeking out time alone is good for your sanity – be that standing on top of a mountain and breathing in the clean air, having a quiet cup of coffee in your favourite hideaway, or sitting under a tree for an afternoon while reading a book and enjoying every single minute of it. Being alone means doing things by yourself and also doing them *for* yourself.

By contrast, if you feel lonely, somebody else's company will help to put a smile on your face or distract you from your current situation or challenges. Loneliness is the feeling of needing others around you but, for whatever reason, you are unable to fill that gap. The gap here can, in turn, become a void and more of an aching loss or feeling that something is missing.

Sadly, for some, loneliness can become all consuming. It's one of the most significant challenges facing the older generation, where ill health or mobility problems prevent ease of access to others, resulting in lost companionship and an overwhelming feeling of isolation.

You will agree with some of the following definitions, while others won't resonate for you. Do you recognise yourself in any of these? Highlight the ones that you resonate with most. Are they where you want to be or do you need to make changes?

Loneliness	✓/✗	Being Alone	✓/✗
Isolation with expectations unmet.		Finding a sense of freedom in isolation.	
Crying without being seen.		Being so at ease with yourself that you smile or laugh for no reason.	
Emotional abandonment.		Physical and mental freedom.	
Makes you want to find distractions to free yourself from it.		Allows you to follow your heart.	
Stems from blaming yourself.		Comes from loving yourself.	
The feeling of being disconnected.		Connecting with yourself.	
The riot in your brain that nobody can hear.		The quiet everyone can feel but you don't need to share.	
Depending on someone else for happiness.		Finding happiness on your own.	
Longing for something that doesn't exist.		Enjoying everything that exists in solitude.	
Rooted in fear.		Rooted in peace.	
Being restless all the time.		Being content with yourself.	

There are no right or wrong answers here. Your observations and reflections are exactly that – your observations. You don't need to share them; interpret them as you see fit. The challenge here is to understand whether you're alone as opposed to lonely.

Make a daily appointment with yourself to either spend time alone or enjoy your time alone by reading, writing, meditating, thinking or just breathing. You can get stronger and build resilience through 'me time'.

Where are you feeling isolated?

It can feel incredibly lonely at the top of your business or department. Everyone wants a piece of you. Everyone wants answers. You have to be the brains and the fixer for everybody. It does not have to feel isolating, but for many, that's the way it is.

However, isolation can happen at all levels in business. As careers progress, individuals climb further away from that team environment where everyone is equal. The common goal is to do a good job and hopefully get a promotion or a transfer to the next level. If something goes wrong, you ask a colleague. Everybody looks out for each other, and in the main you all work, play and support each other.

Then the promotions come along, and everyone wants answers. Answers to all the questions that, two or three months ago, you didn't know and potentially still don't know. So what do you do now? Do you fib and risk being found out later? Do you guess and risk getting it hopelessly wrong? Do you risk being demoted because you messed up? You can't possibly ask for help because people might think you're not good enough to do the job. These are all signs of 'imposter syndrome', the fear of being found out for not being good enough. This can be the foundation for feelings of isolation.

In one of my early roles at a global bank, there was a manager who suffered terribly from everything I have just described. She had been promoted above her level of competence and confidence, and with that came an inability to perform, which sadly led to a lack of respect from her colleagues. In the end she was left feeling isolated, hating every day at work. It affected her health, so she quit.

Some might say this only occurs if you lack adequate training in the role. Unfortunately, people are still promoted without being given the skills and tools to do the job. Of course, not everyone who is promoted feels abandoned, but the feeling of isolation can increase as you go up the ladder. With a great team around you, the outcomes can be far more positive.

Why are you so afraid of not looking perfect all the time, not having all the answers? Why can't you be vulnerable and say that you don't know everything? Sadly, some people do wish to see you fail. You know the people I mean – the empire-builders, the schemers – those people whose integrity markers are totally out of line with yours.

The good news is that life tends to balance out in the long run, and those who play games will eventually get caught out. I could quote stories of fake politicians, the school bully or the snake oil used car salesperson, but they won't help your motivation to stay true to your personal code of conduct. When you need advice, support or appropriate training, it is your responsibility to ask.

There is no long-term benefit to imprisoning yourself in a world of isolation; we are social creatures and we need love and interaction. This is where your mental wealth team will step in. Nobody has to work, live or exist in isolation. The dangers include reduced productivity and performance, fear of taking action, depression, procrastination and avoidance of situations that involve interaction and questions. Learning how to ask for help and who to ask for help from is the solution – and this is what your mental wealth team can provide.

In my corporate finance days I had phone lines installed into my house so that I could work remotely. It was a massive thing for the company to trust members of the team to work away from the main office, where control and discipline was easier to enforce. Today we are all attached by the umbilical cord of digital technology and being remote doesn't make a difference to our ability to work.

I think the question has to be asked: is this a change for the better or worse? Is it increasing people's feelings of isolation?

Digital overload poses a serious challenge to a sensible work–life balance. How many people carry two phones, one business, one personal plus a tablet or laptop? Add to that the ability for everything to be accessible from the cloud. Being in the office, stuck in a traffic jam on the motorway or even on holiday, we are potentially always on call!

When was the last time you experienced total remoteness, with no digital interaction or electronic screens to distract or entertain you? With digital freedom, your outlook changes and maybe you will discover creativity for fun, adventures or new hobbies.

A few years ago I went on holiday to Newfoundland, off the east coast of Canada. It was stunning, beautiful and remote. At that time, when I walked off the plane and turned on my mobile, there was no service, so I had two weeks in digital isolation.

For the first two days, I twitched and stressed, and managed to arrange access via the main reception to check in with the office in case of an emergency. After that, I relaxed into what was one of the best holidays I've ever had. It took being totally remote to allow me to truly reconnect with my family, reboot my mental wellbeing and return home a very motivated person.

There are times when positive isolation really can help the mind, body and soul. If you have just the one phone, would a second for personal use allow you to switch off more effectively from work at the weekend? Answering emails at 11pm or 5.30am might be efficient, but it's not good for you in the long term. If you need help in reducing your digital dependency, then ask for it. Being available 24/7 is a habit, but having a balanced life is also a habit. If that is not the case for you today, then make it a target!

One of the best ways of achieving this is through positive collaborations. We all need to find like-minded people to help us achieve more than we can on our own.

One person working in isolation can achieve a finite amount in a day, a week or a year. However, the old saying that 'two heads are better than one' is undoubtedly true; one person can stimulate different thinking to another working in a blinkered silo. From various viewpoints come ideas and innovation, which in turn can unleash greatness and creativity.

For me, there is a simple question to answer: am I the best person to complete the task?

- If the answer is no, collaborate.

- If the answer is yes, calculate at what cost, time, energy, budget and sacrifices.

Reality check here! Quite often the challenge is not that you don't want to bring in other people; it's the perception that by asking for help or bringing in others, you become in some way weaker or less brilliant because you cannot do it on your own. Is this about your ego and awareness, or is it really a simple case of knowing what is and isn't a practical use of your energy and effort? Ego in this context refers to your self-reflection and how you view your strengths and weaknesses, rather than the ego of a narcissistic politician with a misguided and over-inflated belief in their own importance and abilities.

Translate this into your environment and current working practices. How often do you choose to work alone? Let me rephrase that. How often do you choose not to take advice, support or input from others (collaborate) and therefore choose to work on your own? It's unlikely you had to go back too far in your memory bank to recall an occasion when you were guilty of this – we all do it.

Ask yourself: am I the best at creative thinking? Am I the best at following a process or completing a specific task? Am I the best at finishing a task in hand? If the answer is anything but a 100% confirmation that you are the best, who is better, who has a different experience, who has been in your shoes before and could know something you don't? Ask those questions then choose to take action and seek that person out. If you are feeling isolated, is it because you are choosing not to collaborate?

Understanding your 'why'

Purpose, direction, goal-setting and understanding your 'why' are often talked about in relation to professional and self-development. Where do you want to go? Without a clear direction, how can you leave a legacy? How do you define happiness?

Several years ago, with the help of my good friend David Hyner (more from him on goals a little later), I wrote down my purpose. I'm sharing it here to give you some context. Some elements are less relevant now than they were at the time of writing. And, for your information, a copy of this has been carried in my wallet ever since it was created.

> To be a best friend, colleague, father and husband whose actions mirror his words, giving a sense of personal pride and peace within. A role model to my children and looking after those I love and love me. While being forgiving of mine and others' imperfections, constantly learning, innovating and providing adventures every day, every holiday, in everything that I do.

This definition is not perfect, but it has helped my direction and focus. If ever I am lost or struggling for direction, a quick read-through and I am reminded of where I want to be heading. I regularly imagine living life as though it's a long, long holiday, managing the ups and downs while having fun along the way, surrounded by a mental wealth team that evolves and adapts as life moves along.

There is a beautiful poem called 'The Dash', by Linda Ellis, which is often read out at funerals. It focuses on the dash between two dates – the day you are born and the time you die. What would you like to be said about you in your obituary, about your dash? Try writing it down now and see how it reads back to you.

The poem reminds me of this quote: 'The two most important days in your life are the day you are born, and the day you find out why.' What would happen if you refocused your mind on why you are here while including a focus on fun, enjoyment, love, friendship and community in your life, rather than just getting by and existing?

Thinking about my desire to live life as though it were a long holiday, wouldn't it be great to live your life as if it were a permanent holiday? I was first introduced to this way of thinking by my coach, Martin Goodyer. It's such a simple idea, but that doesn't mean to say it's easy to put into practice.

They say that perception is in the eye of the beholder, so why not view 80 years of life as an 80-year holiday? That has to be better than 80 years of trials, chores and challenges. Sure, there will be good times and bad, even on holiday, but what would that do to your mindset if you were trying to be on holiday in your head, rather than trying to make it to the weekend or just paying a few more bills?

Over an average 80-year life, we have 700,800 hours to use as we choose (24 hours x 365 days x 80 years = 700,800 hours). During that time we spend:

- up to 26 years asleep – more than 200,000 hours

- 45 years at work for eight hours a day, 220 days per year = more than 90,000 hours; in total – up to 50% of these hours are taken up with meetings

- a year and a half of our lives on the commute to and from work

- according to some research, 368 days in the pub – which is an underestimate for some people I know

- only 15% of an average life going to school, even though many of us never stop learning.

There are other weird statistics that can be found online about the number of hours spent during a lifetime on the toilet, eating food, sitting on a bus, arguing, crying or smiling and many more.

We change our approach when it comes to planning our holidays; the average person has four or five weeks per year, be that a vacation away from home or a staycation. That's 400 weeks over a lifetime, which equates to 2,800 days. Travel agents and travel journalists claim we spend up to 30 hours planning in great detail everything we want to see, taste and experience, demonstrating the importance we place on creating a happy holiday.

If you were to plan your 80-year holiday, your dash, or your life in advance, where would you start and how would you do it? Holidays are generally associated with happiness, memories and experiences. There are many factors that will bring you joy and contentment. I am challenging your thinking, to help you identify where you are using up precious time with apathy, laziness or fear.

There are people who always appear to be happy and have a cheerful glow about them; perhaps they have adapted this mindset and take joy in every moment as if they were on some sort of permanent holiday.

Time for some internal reflection. Rate yourself in the following areas on how well you currently experience joy and happiness (see table overleaf). You can use any rating system – Gold, Silver, Bronze, 1–10, Red, Green, Amber – whatever works for you. The second part is for you to add in what you choose to improve, adapt or change as per the examples included.

Small steps cumulatively make a massive difference to your mindset and sense of wellbeing. You have the power to make decisions about your direction.

With your mental wealth team behind you, decision-making becomes easier and your journey becomes less of a rollercoaster ride with better-managed highs and lows.

	Rate
Relationships: Express your heart. People who have close friendships are happier due to their ability to express genuine interest in what people say, in a way that enriches relationships and cultivates positive emotions. **I choose...** to put my phone down when I am talking to someone else and give them my full attention.	
Acts of kindness: Cultivate kindness. People who volunteer or simply care for others consistently seem to be happier. **I choose...** to perform one random act of kindness for a stranger every day.	
Exercise and physical wellbeing: Keep moving and eat well. Regular exercise is associated with improved mental wellbeing and a lower incidence of depression and poor mental health. **I choose...** to exercise three times a week, go for a walk or complete a couch-to-5km.	
Flow: If you are deeply involved in trying to reach a goal or an activity that is challenging and well suited to your skills, you experience a joyful state called flow, which means doing what you do because you like what you're doing. **I choose...** to allow myself time for a new hobby.	
Spiritual engagement and meaning: Spiritual and religious practice can lead to happiness. Spirituality is closely related to the discovery of greater meaning in our lives. **I choose...** to find a new yoga instructor.	
Strengths and virtues: The happiest people are those who have discovered their unique strengths and virtues and use them for a purpose that is greater than their personal goals. **I choose...** to double what I raised last year for my favourite charity.	
Growth mindset, optimism, mindfulness and gratitude: Grateful people are tuned into positive emotions and experience a greater sense of belonging. **I choose...** to learn how to play the bagpipes.	
What else? **I choose...**	

Building Your Mental Wealth Team

As discussed in the introduction to this book, the benefits of combining your mental health regime with your mental wealth team can have a considerable impact on your life.

The team has four main categories: you and your self-care, your coach, your professional support team and your mastermind group – not forgetting committed family and friends who will all play their roles.

These are the pillars that hold up your ceiling; all are equally important to your mental wealth. Every individual will dedicate different amounts of effort to each pillar, and you may take away more from one section than the others. My hope is to help you improve your outlook and build a mental wealth team that supports you in all your endeavours.

Self-care: Looking after Number One

Self-care is about making yourself a priority and developing physical and mental approaches that will sustain you. A balance between body and mind is so important for your long-term success and prosperity; these two things are interlinked and you can't have one without the other.

Self-care is about consciously and intentionally keeping your mental and physical self in peak condition – most of the time. Perfection doesn't exist, so you will not always get this right. Optimum self-care is built on whatever you do to take care of yourself physically, emotionally, psychologically, nutritionally and spiritually.

Throughout your life there are many times when you could take better care of yourself, yet how often do you block out personal time in your diary to make this happen? Just imagine having a support network that looks after your mental wellbeing, physical health and nutrition, so you are in peak condition more of the time and able to have more fun.

The first step is to make yourself number one in your world. This might sound obvious but to many (including myself) it isn't. The realisation that I wasn't number one in my own head, in spite of all my knowledge and personal insights, was hugely enlightening to me. Everybody else in the family always came first, even the dog. All my planning, interests and personal challenges, according to me, had to be completed outside of normal family time and at minimal inconvenience to my family.

Even business trips, playing golf or visiting other friends have always been completed with the mindset of creating minimal impact on my family – because they come first, not me. Family life does not work without give and take; there has to be a balance found between living in the moment and the teenage approach that has one singular focus – to get to the end of a day with no consideration for anyone else.

Being number one requires a greater focus on being present. Clearly age brings wisdom, knowledge and responsibilities, which can prevent that perceived selfish approach to life. Does that help you become the best version of you? I don't think it always does. Knowing that I haven't made myself number one explains some of the personal side effects on my mental health, mindset and wellbeing. It certainly highlights some of the pressures I put myself under, which in turn impact on my moods, productivity and hunger, so the answer is yes, I am now a better version of myself.

The people you choose to support you and your self-care can make a real difference to how well you look after yourself and where you are on your own priority list. Putting yourself first is the correct order in life: you can't look after your family, pets and friends if you are not fit for purpose. Caring for yourself initially requires substantial mental and physical effort, but once you have developed your routine and habits, it will become second nature.

Your mind

How you look after your mind in terms of self-care will help you investigate more closely what is in your control and what really isn't helping you. A specific objective is to understand that the actions you take are your responsibility, as is your approach to fun, enjoying the moment, spontaneity and taking time for yourself, all the while considering the relationships that bring you value and assistance. There are many choices to be made about what you want to do now, the direction you wish to head in, or the decision to stay where you are.

The importance of gratitude

In 2014, I had the privilege of working with Stephen Sutton, a young man from Birmingham who had been diagnosed with terminal cancer, having already beaten cancer three times before. He talked about the much-written-about number 86,400, the number of seconds we have in a day. You can't buy any extras, that's your lot. How you use them is your choice, and when they have gone, they have gone forever.

When I interviewed Stephen, he said: 'No one can buy me any more time. I can only achieve more with the time I have left.' Three weeks later he died, having raised over £6m for his chosen charity, the Teenage Cancer Trust. People lined the streets during the funeral of this truly inspirational young man, and yellow ribbons were festooned all over the town where he lived, in tribute to him.

I'm sharing his story to focus your mind on how you choose to reflect on your triumphs and failures every day, week or year. At the end of the day, do you reflect and replay in your mind all the little frustrations? If you do, why? It might be consciously or even subconsciously, and the chances are that you replay the harmful rubbish over and over again in your mind. Why not reframe and focus on the good things? A baby's giggle will always make you smile. You know the sound... you're probably smiling right now. Create a daily routine that reinforces the positive activities, memories and enjoyment. Here are a few suggestions you might like to add to your self-care routine:

Daily gratitude journal: A subtle but significant difference to a normal journal is that you write everything and anything that makes you feel positive. After time it should help you revel in your daily gratitude and focus on the health, wealth, wisdom and positive emotions you felt as a result.

Dear diary: Here, you can reflect on all the things you have done or felt during the day; it doesn't have to be any more complicated than that. People's innermost thoughts are squirrelled away in diaries, and reading them can be hugely enlightening. After my mother passed away, I found her diary and learnt so much more about the challenges she faced in her life after being paralysed by childhood polio. She never really spoke openly about it so I felt privileged to read her diary. Writing about events and your feelings about them can be extremely cathartic and a great way of unburdening yourself.

Positives diary: Several years ago, when my wife lost her mother to cancer, she wrote one positive memory per day in her diary for the following year. On the anniversary of her mum's death, she had 365 positive memories to look back on and celebrate. It can be as simple as just one word every day – there's no need to overcomplicate it.

Positive pictures: After my own mum's passing, I preferred to take a photograph that made me smile: the cat with a moustache like Poirot, the icicle that looked like a face, or the unique shape of dog poo on the footpath. Life can be hard, but everywhere around us there are pictures to be taken and positive memories to be created and stored. At the end of that year, I had 365 positive photographs to look back on that made me smile.

Coffee and sweat: Up at 4.30am, large espresso and off to the gym. Either you'll enjoy this idea or laugh at it; the point is that it's a positive routine for certain people and if it works for you, keep on doing it.

Cold-water swimming: I know that if I lived nearer the sea I would likely be one of those people who took regular dips. Whether I'd do it daily or all year round is a different question. For many, it's a daily routine that has proved to be therapeutic and encouraged positive mental health.

Focusing more on daily experiences will enable you to recognise the great things that are going on around you all of the time. Subconsciously you will start focusing on the positive. Yes, some days will be harder, and that's where your mental wealth team comes into play. It's not just about sharing doom and gloom and problems; your network will appreciate the funny stories as well. Who knows? Maybe your life could resemble an 80-year holiday and be turned into a blockbuster movie in the future.

Healthy, wealthy, wise

I was recently talking to a close friend of mine who was having a BMW (a bitch, moan and whine) about everything wrong in his world. He was playing the victim. It was quite a sad conversation as I didn't think he had much to moan about. He just took pleasure in whining. I asked him a potent set of questions that I ask myself when I'm feeling a bit fed up.

- Are you healthy?

- Are you wealthy?

- Are you wise?

If you can respond yes to all of them, then the question is: do you really have a reason to whine?

My friend's answers were a stuttering yes to all three questions. He is healthy, aside from a back problem that was probably caused by the excess weight he was carrying. Yes, he is wealthy – he owns a lovely house in a great neighbourhood. Though it might not be as big as some other people's houses, it is still pretty significant. He is wise, educated, with a good job and the love of his partner and child, who are also healthy.

How many people do we know who desire all of that and can't get anywhere near it? There are times when some will answer yes to each question without feeling good about everything else in their lives, and when this happens it's our responsibility to ask better questions; we do not know what else is going on in the background (more on questions later).

I was recently introduced to the '5 Ss' used by a psychologist contact who is based at Broadmoor high security prison in the UK. I'm sharing them here as they might trigger more insights:

- ♟ Sleep – are you getting enough? Do you need more?

- ♟ Substance – eg alcohol / drugs – are you having too much or too little?

- ♟ Social – are you getting any social interaction? Do you need more? Do you need less (me time)?

- ♟ Stress – are you stressed? About what? Can you share it to relieve some stress? What can be done to reduce your stress?

- ♟ Sustenance – are you eating well and keeping fit and healthy?

Bringing the 5 Ss into balance can help individuals get back to normality. When isolated, many people can lack sleep and social interaction, and find themselves overcompensating by consuming too much alcohol and creating more stress.

When the focus is on material wealth and status symbols, we forget the things that truly matter and ignore what we already have. We have all lost friends and family to illnesses such as cancer. When tragedies come out of the blue, it can require a great deal of time for recovery and support and you may not be able to answer yes to the healthy, wealthy and wise questions.

This is the time to seek external help from people with relevant expertise. We can always add to our self-care team when the need arises; bereavement and grief counsellors are such a valuable resource. No one should be on their own in these circumstances, however long they last.

If the answer to any of the healthy, wealthy and wise questions is no, talk to your team. They know and understand you, and can offer support and advice. By contrast, if you can say yes to all of these questions, remember you have a moral duty to reach out and help others.

Taking responsibility for your actions

When you were a child, how often did your parents tell you that you had to take responsibility for your actions? How, if you did X, then Y would happen and not to be surprised when everything went wrong? Did you ever learn that lesson? How often do things play out differently from how you wanted them to?

These scenarios remind me of the 1998 film *Sliding Doors,* starring Gwyneth Paltrow and John Hannah. It describes how different one person's life might have been had they taken a different path; more specifically, had they not missed that early train home. The film cleverly plays out both experiences in parallel so we can watch the impact on this woman's life caused by that one, critical, missed train.

How often have you wondered how things might have turned out if something had not happened, or asked yourself the question, 'What if?' Whether you are a fatalist or believe in serendipity is irrelevant; at some point, circumstances conspired to put you where you are today – be that good, bad or indifferent.

I believe that you are somehow responsible for everything that goes on in your life. In many situations, the domino effect could have started years ago, and you are only seeing them fall today. Don't spend too much time focusing on the negative and blaming yourself for what goes wrong, or actions that you took in the past. Why not try looking at it from another angle?

Look at the good that manifests every day as a result of your actions. If you choose to take responsibility for the positive things that happen every day, which generally get forgotten, ignored or go unnoticed, there are good things to focus on all of the time. If all that goes right in your world is your fault, then do more of it. Take responsibility for the good that takes place in your life every day, as it will help it become so much richer and more fulfilling.

Reflecting on the progress you have made in a month can be healthy for your confidence and self-esteem. Conversely, self-flagellation for a weak-performing month can have adverse effects. One of the foundations of behavioural change is that if there isn't an emotional connection to what you want to change, then nothing different will happen. It takes a huge amount of self-awareness and energy to spot the signals by yourself. This is why you need a good mental wealth team watching out for you with the necessary awareness to recognise when things are going wrong or likely to go wrong.

Sadly, without support this can go on for years and result in what Richard Wilkins (the UK's self-appointed Minister of Inspiration) refers to, ironically, as an NLE – a Near Life Experience – where years evaporate with little forward momentum or achievement.

For the month about to start, choose a couple of things that you will commit to seeing all the way through. Start small and build the habit, e.g. commit to being home to put the kids to bed, commit to half an hour's exercise five times a week, take a walk at lunchtime every day or meditate daily for 10 minutes.

There is no point in trying to change everything at any one time as you are more likely to fail; never set yourself up to fail. Aim instead for small stepping stones of cumulative action. By taking responsibility for your actions and remaining dedicated to your choices, you will be able to see gradual positive changes.

Calling Dr Fun

All too often, we focus on the serious stuff – on getting things done, earning money and considering the consequences of our actions (or inaction). When are we meant to sit down and have fun, enjoy ourselves and play? If you created a Dr Fun avatar, what would it look like, how would it behave and how different would it be from the current you?

There is a passage in the Bible that resonates with me. You may be surprised to have Mike Pagan quoting the scriptures at you, but I have to admit this was brought to my attention when watching that fantastic 1980s film *Footloose*, with Kevin Bacon. He quotes the following verses when arguing that the young people of the town should be allowed to dance. At that point in the story, dancing was illegal due to the belief that it encouraged excess fun, leading to drinking and potential promiscuity.

A Time for Everything

For everything there is a season,
a time for every activity under heaven.
A time to be born and a time to die.
A time to plant and a time to harvest.
A time to kill and a time to heal.
A time to tear down and a time to build up.
A time to cry and a time to laugh.
A time to grieve and a time to dance.
A time to scatter stones and a time to gather stones.
A time to embrace and a time to turn away.
A time to search and a time to quit searching.
A time to keep and a time to throw away.
A time to tear and a time to mend.
A time to be quiet and a time to speak.
A time to love and a time to hate.
A time for war and a time for peace.

– Ecclesiastes 3: 1–8 (New Living Translation)

A time for everything. Whether or not you follow a faith, it provides a compelling philosophy to live your life by. It covers almost every part of your life, including the positive and negative situations you'll inevitably have to deal with.

The area we rarely focus on is a time to laugh – i.e. playtime. When it comes to organising fun, we tend to leave it to the last minute, forget or become distracted by something more 'urgent' that crops up. It's up to you to increase your playtime. When did you last do the following?

- **Have a delicious belly laugh, to the point that it hurt.**

- **Go out on a date night with your partner.**

- **Take up a new sport, go back to an old sport, coach a sport you've always loved, or learn to become a coach.**

- **Enrol in online or evening classes – whatever brings you joy, be it cookery, languages, flower arranging or optimising your smartphone.**

- Set a physical, fitness, weight or personal challenge, committing money and a buddy to it so you can't quit.

- Get to the cinema, theatre, restaurant or concert.

- Join an amateur dramatic society, singing club or art appreciation society.

- Have a monthly get-together, dinner party or excursion with a different theme.

- Let your hair down and splash in puddles?

- Notice yourself smiling. A smile is infectious and is generally returned by the people you meet.

Are you a fun person to be around? How often do you laugh? I have created a laughter diary because it puts a smile on my face several times a day. Note down two or three things daily that made you laugh out loud – not an internal chuckle, but a proper audible laugh. On some days you may find this challenging as there won't seem to be much to laugh about. Try looking harder: the funny emoji, the comments made by a child, the Homer Simpson moment spoken by a colleague, the TV show that just gets you. By putting laughter on your radar and making a note of the funny moments in your life, you will notice more laughter, and because of that, you will laugh more.

All of this takes effort; there will be times when you will not have the energy, budget or desire to see it through. However, I promise you that at the end of the year you will be laughing, smiling, more energised and happier because you have a list of new memories and stories to tell. I know you work hard – let's see if you can play harder.

Time for spontaneity

Do you need to unlock the door to a little more spontaneity? What would you do if you had no one to report back to, had complete carte blanche to do whatever you wanted for fun right now? What could you do spontaneously today?

There are various stages in life where you enjoy a greater or lesser amount of spontaneity, or a problem occurs when you forget how to tap into your naturally impulsive personality. Not everything has to be scripted. What would happen if you just went for it?

Be spontaneous and do something fun, different, creative or maybe even naughty (I didn't say illegal). Go on, treat yourself to some more fun today. It's unlikely to kill you and may well help you laugh more – especially if you've spent too much time crying. Although it might sound counterintuitive, you need to plan for spontaneity by creating the time, space and environment in which it can happen.

Rest, relaxation, playtime and family fun need to be on your radar. At the end of the day, life is for living so we should make time to live! When, and how, can you take time out in such a way that it doesn't affect your business and makes you stronger, bolder, braver and more capable of taking on the world?

Life is not meant to be dull, drab and the same old thing; it needs to be inventive and creative to make it stimulating and enjoyable. The illness of presenteeism in the corporate world is outdated and has no place in the modern working world. There is always someone whose car is the last in the car park at the end of the day, who is physically present in the office, even though their mind switched off many hours ago.

In the new world of working remotely and digitally, how will you bring more spontaneity into your working day and mindset? You can choose how to set the environment that is best for you, so choose one that stimulates your mind and creativity. If this doesn't come naturally to you, seek out input from your mental wealth team.

Take time for you

The outcome of taking time for you is the creation of a positive mental state. Take a trip away from home, escape to the countryside or find sanctuary in your favourite coffee shop. If you don't make it happen, it won't. I have done a great deal of writing while sitting in the corner of a cafe wearing headphones that drown out the rest of the world.

One of the environments in which I take time for myself is on long-haul flights. I realise many will link this to the romance of travel and exploration, but for me it's more fundamental than that. With a set of headphones on, in the confines of my seat, my laptop and few distractions, I can get so much done – from writing and development to crafting and creating, and then watching a film with a glass of wine. It's incredible what I can achieve. Then, while I am away, I continue this focus of getting stuff done, researching more material and investigating more opportunities.

Try taking some time each day to do something different. Here is a 31-day planner, with examples of possible activities that might stimulate some action – some will need you to be number one, which may be a challenge in itself!

1 Get outside	**2** Sleep during the day	**3** Help a stranger	**4** Change your state	**5** Share something dear to you
6 Play with a baby	**7** Yoga / Pilates	**8** Sponsor a friend	**9** Make that decision – Just Do It	**10** Try a new playlist
11 Meal prep with others	**12** Spend time with the elderly	**13** Spring clean somewhere	**14** Pamper your body	**15** Phone a neglected contact
16 Laughter hour	**17** Lunch out	**18** Enjoy nature	**19** Gratitude journal	**20** Abandon one toxin
21 Join a club/ class	**22** Have a catch-up coffee	**23** Read a different book	**24** Try a new hobby – singing/art?	**25** New food – healthy or special
26 Take some me-time	**27** Throw two things away	**28** Take a group exercise class	**29** Serve up a date night	**30** Random act of kindness
31 Meditate on a hill				

What have you learnt? Can you take more time for you? Do you feel any different? How are your energy levels? Have you noticed any changes in your state of mind? There are no instruction manuals that work for everyone – experiment until you find the areas that work best for your positive state of mind.

Manage the Mood Hoovers

Life becomes so much easier and more fun when we are surrounded by positive people and become immune to the effects of negative personalities. For many years I have talked and written about the Mood Hoovers – people who, no matter what the situation, suck up any happy feelings you have and leave you feeling drained.

Other names for these people are Energy Vampires and Dream Stealers. You have probably just visualised someone in your life – that's how powerful they are!

What are the common traits of these negatively charged people, and how can we cope with them more effectively? If we accomplish that, then surely our lives would be filled with joy without that rain cloud of doom following us around? Wishful thinking, I hear you say. However, is it? You are in control of what you think, who you hang out with, where you play and what you choose to do, so giving these people a wide berth is within your control.

The challenge is to manage them, so they don't poison the atmosphere, your productivity or your success. When it comes to self-care, you need to be selective about the company you keep, because empathy only goes so far without it becoming a drain on you. Here are some simple tactics to use when appropriate:

- Walking away isn't possible in every situation but it's often the right thing for your self-care.

- Don't take their call in the first place – swipe left.

- If you have accepted a call and find that you need to remove yourself from a negative situation, put them on hold or say you're going into a tunnel (obvious, I know, but it works).

- Resist offering guidance. Instead, give them back control. Say: 'I'm confident you'll be able to find the right answer on your own,' then move along.

In my family, we have interventions where we can all chat, everyone has a voice and nothing is judged. We address our troubles and the negative energy in the household. Following the conversations, appropriate action is taken, ill-serving habits are addressed and harmony is restored.

You need to be aware of individuals who are causing you issues, even if they are family, so you can respond with your best interests in mind.

When it comes to negative talk it's easy to point the finger. However, the most negative person in your life can often be inside your own head. You would never let anybody else speak to you the way that little voice does.

We all have sh*t to deal with in our lives, whether that be health, a global pandemic, taxes or a boiler breakdown. Make a clear choice about how you manage negativity.

One technique I learnt from my mental wealth team was Karpman's drama triangle: victim, rescuer and persecutor. These are some of the roles people unconsciously play, or try to manipulate other people into playing. I have heard my daughter quoting this to her friends in challenging times where they have been creating unnecessary dramas.

The people that live inside the drama triangle can fluctuate between roles, depending on the situation. If there is no crisis looming on the horizon, they will create or manifest one. They can be incredibly tiring to work or live with as they are high maintenance and needy. The good news is it's not a lifelong condition; people will go through these phases, and with the help of a coach they can become aware of their behaviours and change their approach. However, without that awareness, it could be years before they understand what's going on.

Everyone is influenced by those around them, including the Mood Hoovers and the Dynamos (see below), but our responses to their presence can vary. Eric Berne's transactional analysis (TA) theory states that we take on a role in response to a situation we are in. TA refers to the three ego states – parent, adult and child. At any given time we can take on one of these roles when we interact with other people. The desired state is to be in an adult-to-adult environment where both are equal; however, should one person assume the parent ego they automatically put the other person into the child ego, which may or may not be well received. These relationships become a drain on your energy and can negatively affect your performance. Over time, the individual can become one of your Mood Hoovers.

It's much more fun to focus on the positive people in our lives – the ones that exude energy and dynamism. These are the people you always look forward to hearing from or meeting up with. You see their name pop up on your phone and it puts a smile on your face; or you always seek them out at an event as you know they are great fun. I am not talking about romantic connections – these are people whom you respect, admire and feel good to know.

Picture someone you love to be around. They might be a friend at the rugby club, a mum from the school run or the managing director of that creative and intelligent new business. What exactly do they have and what would you call it? I'd call it 'va-va-voom'. These are the connections where you are equal in standing, neither of you talks down to the other or seeks permission from the other in any way and you walk away from your encounters feeling uplifted.

What effect would these Dynamos have on you? These are the people who always make things happen and spending more time with them will subconsciously have a positive influence on you. You can pick up behaviours, qualities and, most importantly, attitudes which can motivate and inspire you to act differently. Conversely, of course, you know only too well what the effects can be of spending too much time with Mood Hoovers!

When I ooze positivity, I can carry people along with me, and because I am flying at full speed, others want to get involved. Moods come and go, energy ebbs and flows, so you need to be aware of the impact you can have on others.

It is worth considering my late mother-in-law's advice about friendships. I was able to relate to it and it has stuck with me ever since. Some people are with us for a season, a reason or for life. When it is the end of their time with you, let them go and enjoy remembering the time you had together in that season or the reason they were with you. By contrast, treasure the lifers; their friendship will ebb and flow through highs and lows and, at the end of the day, they will always be there for you.

Over the next 12 months, my challenge to you is to manage or even remove the Mood Hoovers in your life and seek out more Dynamos. Learn from them, discover their habits and behaviours; you may even uncover a new lifelong friendship.

Finding your tribe

Do the people you associate with support your self-care regime? Do they add value, bring you joy or uplift you? Where is your community or tribe? Do you have a group of like-minded people with whom you can share stories, challenges and thinking?

A few years ago when my teenage daughter was struggling with certain friendships at school, I gave her a picture with a quote on it from Dame Helen Mirren, who said: 'My only regret in life is not telling more people to f*** off.' She was referring to the fake, shallow and false relationships that come and go, and I felt it was a good message for my daughter at that time.

The message for all of us is to be discerning about the type of people we want to work and spend time with. Consider the role models you choose or have chosen in the past because of their inspirational approach or triumphs over adversity.

When I hear the words dedication and resilience, I am reminded of an intimate acoustic concert my daughter and I attended several years ago with the rock legend Brian May, the lead guitarist from the band Queen – you know, the one with the hair! The man has an obscene amount of talent, and I do mean that positively. The event was simply incredible. This is a man who has been dedicated to developing his skill and talent for more than 50 years. A truly positive role model and inspiration for my daughter on her guitar journey.

Many people get their support and interaction from their religious community, associations or book club. That ability to feel comfortable enough to share your thinking and ideas in a safe environment is so important, specifically for masterminding (more on this to follow). In the world of business networking there are many events you can attend. At some you might feel welcome, and that the people in the room get you, whereas others just aren't right for you. That's OK, trust your instincts and don't go back!

Joining a group isn't the final step in overcoming loneliness or the need for kinship – you have to attend as well. A friend of my daughter's at university wasn't settling in well. He'd joined all the clubs and societies that he was interested in and still felt isolated and alone. The problem was he hadn't actually attended the groups or put in any effort to see if they might work for him. It's the same as trying to get fit by joining a gym but never setting foot through the door! Make an effort to find the environment that works for you.

Building positive relationships

As you get older, you'll meet more people through work and other activities, but how often do you make a new best friend? Once a week, once a year, or very rarely? I often see people trying to make new such connections at events, working hard to build that special relationship with the person sitting opposite them, when they only met five minutes before. At the end of the event, what happens? Someone says 'I'll give you a call next week', and nine times out of ten that doesn't happen. Can you honestly say that you have never failed to follow up?

It's just like the dating game – showing all the right signs, chemistry and desire on the first date and promising to call, then not following through.

Be sure to carefully vet and select the people who are worth your investment. How much time, effort and money are you willing to invest in meetings? If the number of meetings you're having doesn't balance with the returns, then you're meeting the wrong people.

I do need to mention rejection here. If you take them personally, the big rejections can hurt. However, in business, nine times out of ten it is not personal. Rejection is part of life; you just have to get on with it. After a rejection, I use just one word: 'Next.' I don't want my focus or productivity to be affected; it is just not worth the anxiety or mental anguish.

Have you ever avoided asking questions because you're afraid of receiving a negative answer? Try keeping a record of the number of times you avoid or put off asking for something. Just thinking about it will help. What, honestly, is the worst that can happen if they say no? Don't fear rejection – focus on the next question you want to ask. The opposite of rejection is approval. Yet many are not able to accept that they have been chosen and not rejected.

How often do you choose to ignore positive statements or deflect compliments? From the polite compliment about your cup of tea and the clothes you are wearing through to a statement from an extremely happy client that you are clearly the best on the planet at what you do. Time and time again, I come across this in the world of communication and presentation coaching. I often meet individuals who refuse to acknowledge their positive side, their magnificent self. They cannot possibly be any good or have a story that deserves to be heard.

I recently worked with a young woman on her speaking skills and confidence. She delivered a great story to her school, balancing gravitas with humour. Overall it was excellent, and her classmates, teachers and friends told her so. But she was having none of it. She didn't believe she was excellent or would ever become any good at speaking.

Why is it that others see us in such a different way from how we see ourselves? Is it our conditioning and self-programming? I find it is down to the individual's quest for perfection and sadly, in their mind, someone else is always better than them. The problem here is that perfection equals 100% and, aside from the odd maths exam, 100% is never achievable in life. An A grade is 80%, which is excellent – so strive for excellence and being the best, most fabulous version of yourself, not perfection.

Paying someone a compliment feels good. It feels even better when the recipient appreciates the compliment. Be that person when someone pays you that compliment. Say thank you, hold your head up high, feel that warm glow inside and start believing it. Learn to absorb positive feedback and compliments; it can make a big difference to your relationships, your self-care and your confidence.

Pay it forward

There are many ways to have a positive effect on the world. 'Pay it forward' means choosing to do something good for someone else without expectation of reward or response. How often are you guilty of giving with one hand while holding out the other, expecting something in return? We all do it – the challenge is to give with an open heart, knowing that somewhere down the track, when you least expect it, someone will do something truly amazing for you. You have nothing to lose and everything to gain!

Many years ago, as a poor student, I met with an old school friend who was running a wine bar in central London. The evening progressed, and the drink was flowing. I'd spent all my money so I prepared to bow out. My friend's response was simple: 'Don't worry, it's on me, you'll do the same for someone else in the future.' Thanks, Hamish. Needless to say, I have done it many times over and will do it again.

This concept was first introduced to me in the movie *Pay It Forward*, based on an 11-year-old American schoolboy called Trevor McKinney, who had a desire to change the world. I highly recommend that you watch it. The story is simple: the boy does three good deeds for three total strangers, and the caveat attached to these strangers receiving his good deed is that they must agree to pay it forward and do three good deeds themselves for three strangers, and so on. Within a very short time, three good deeds become nine, 27, 81 and then thousands across the state, demonstrating the amazing impact that one person can have. I hope this simple message sticks with you and you are able to introduce it into your life, and positively affect many other people's lives.

Your mind: summary

Your approach to self-care is all about the choices you make and the decisions you take. Not every question has obvious answers, but with positive people working with you these choices become clearer and easier. Many of these activities will help you to put yourself first on your priority list.

You now have a fresh approach to re-evaluating your life, the opportunity to change your outlook, become more grateful for what you already have and have a desire to search out the positive every day. By investigating your habits you can remove the unhelpful ones that reduce your levels of fun. Take responsibility for your actions and create time for you and time for others that incorporates more spontaneity into your life.

Focus on positive relationships and let go of the ones that don't serve you. Nurture and enjoy these good relationships and start to pay things forward.

All of this personal reflection might have made you wonder where you sit on the mental health spectrum, or you might have concerns about a friend, family member or colleague. There are many easily accessible mental health questionnaires online. A good general example is the Edinburgh Postnatal Depression Scale, which is designed to generate further questions and conversation. Always remember – if you need help, ask; there are numerous links to UK-based support groups and mental health charities referenced at the end of the book.

How you approach your mind as part of your self-care is within your control. Now it's up to you to choose how and when you will implement what you have discovered.

Your body

Looking after your body is such an important part of your self-care. This is about what you put into your body and how you can get yourself fit for the goals and challenges that lie ahead. I know my performance can be both positively and negatively affected, depending on what has been going on in my life physically as well as what I have been consuming.

Not everyone is interested in the strange weekend warrior activities I get up to. Some people describe me as a bit of a nutter, and that is good. There are many who make my challenges look amateur, which creates either fear, envy or goals in my head. But none of these physical endeavours can be achieved without looking after my body through a sensible, consistent diet and exercise regime.

Personal challenges

I gain so much from personal challenges – they have had such a positive impact on my self-care. The act of trudging step after step after step up the side of a snow- and ice-covered mountain or swimming stroke after stroke after stroke is strangely hypnotic and meditative for me. These challenges aren't for everyone, I know, but long-term success is about persistence; you have to choose challenges that require ongoing dedication.

The key for me is having a team that will provide a collective identity and shared direction. In 2013, I brought together a random bunch of swimmers and created a relay team to swim the English Channel, which involved two years of training and planning.

Only one of us had any experience of open-water swimming, let alone cold-water sea swimming. We were total novices. This was to be an official relay attempt adhering to Channel Swimming Association rules, which meant no wetsuit – just a costume, a hat and a torch.

Once the order of swimmers was set, you had to stick to it no matter how badly someone was doing, and if one person failed in their leg, the team failed. Not forgetting, of course, that Mother Nature decides your fate: the tides and the weather change and the sea is always in charge.

We had a coach who challenged our techniques, styles and swimming efficiency, plus mentors who had been there before and shared their expertise. The paperwork and numbers were all taken care of with complete transparency by one of the team that enjoyed this work.

We had repeated early starts and uncomfortable, cold and miserable swims that could easily have been put off or avoided. The acclimatisation was the hardest part – getting used to swimming in waters of 12-15°C for long periods of time; for the record, a pool is normally heated to 26°C.

Without that level of dedication and training, we risked jeopardising the chances of the team's success, not to mention our own personal survival. We were only as strong as the least prepared swimmer in our team – if one person failed, we all failed. No pressure there, then!

After two years of planning and training, both physically and mentally, we were at our best and completed the Channel Swim. We were the fastest full men's relay team in 2015 – crossing the English Channel in 11 hours 23 minutes.

A massive spring tide almost doubled the distance we were meant to swim, so the 22-mile crossing became 35 miles long. The exhilaration and feeling of success upon achieving our goal was immeasurable. This was a team challenge, supported by a network of many others who directly and indirectly impacted upon our success. Little acts such as Charlie's girlfriend, who worked for a chocolate manufacturer, bringing all sorts of goodies along to training/the race kept us all motivated.

In the sporting world so much progress is made by the approach to training and improvement, including attending offsite training camps. The athletes go away for days or weeks to focus on improving their performance, shaving a few seconds off times, refining accuracy or building physical stamina. This has been proven to be the difference between medals and trophies. The goal in elite sport is to be the absolute best, leaving no stone unturned; nothing is left to chance. The body has to be at its physical peak, the head has to be in the right space and no distraction is allowed to get in the way of this goal.

In my work with professional sportspeople transitioning into new careers and new lives, I was introduced to research completed by the Dame Kelly Holmes Trust. Professor David Lavallee provided scientifically backed evidence of the positive effects of former sportspeople on the workplace. They might start behind others in terms of knowledge, but as they learn the skills and nuances of the business, within two years they are regularly found at the top of their peer group and the general performance of those around them has improved as well. Knowing this, I actively seek out former professional sportspeople to collaborate and work with on many of my projects and client assignments.

What if you took the professional sportsperson's approach in your life and work, mentally and physically tuning yourself to be the absolute best in that interview or that sales meeting? Average is never the goal: what could you achieve if you aimed to be better than average in all of your pursuits? What new levels of success could you uncover?

Stepping up

Step after step after step – every step takes you in a direction; which direction you choose is up to you. In 2019, along with my race partner Chris Cooper, I took on the Great Kindrochit Quadrathlon challenge. This is said to be the hardest one-day endurance race in Scotland. We swam (1 mile), ran (18 miles), kayaked (8 miles) and cycled (35 miles) in, on and around Loch Tay, surrounded by its monstrous Munros.

To put this into perspective, Snowdon is the highest mountain in Wales at 1,085m. Every Munro in Scotland is more than 1,000m high, and we ran up, ran down and scrambled up and over SEVEN of them! I'm not a runner, and certainly not a fell-runner. Going up and down mountains is just not me. It took us 10 hours to complete just the run, covering a total of 18 miles – that's three-quarters of a marathon just on the mountains fell-running – ouch.

All the race participants understood that it wasn't just about getting to the top of the Munro. Once you got to the top of each one, you knew that you had to come down and then do it all again. This was where it became a problem for me – my knees do not enjoy downhills, so every single step became more painful to the point where I would slide down on my bottom, dodging rocks and sheep mess on the way.

By contrast, my partner Chris enjoyed the running. He jumped down the hillsides like a gazelle with a smile on his face. His challenge was the swim – one mile of open-water swimming across a loch where the temperature of the water was 10 degrees at best! Six months before the event, Chris couldn't swim front crawl. I'm not the fastest swimmer; my strength is swimming for a long period of time – that was the easy bit for me.

We worked together as a buddy team supporting each other through the year of training. We built our stamina and fitness, running from 5 km to 5 miles to 10 km and so on, all off road; and in the pool from two lengths to 20 lengths to 200 lengths. Not forgetting, of course, the need to ride a bike and learn how to kayak in a tandem. I forgot to mention we also had to learn map-reading as well! The Quadrathlon is a race that is completed in pairs due to the high risks and potential safety issues on top of the mountains, from white-out conditions, low cloud and zero visibility. I did say this wasn't easy and maybe a little bit crazy!

So why would anybody do something like this and how can this be even vaguely relevant to self-care? The answer for me is simple: some people love to set practical goals and enjoy the feeling when they achieve them. My goals are physical: the summit of a mountain, the finish line in a race, or landing on foreign soil.

That achievement provides me with a real sense of being ALIVE, a pure adrenaline rush. I don't race to win. I am far too long in the tooth to be trying to win these events – I get involved to complete, not compete. On top of everything else, the taste of that first celebratory beer once the event is over is just gorgeous and well earned.

It is all about stepping up to the challenge of looking after yourself, in whatever form that may be, embracing the theory of my wonderful and effervescent speaking friend, the late Joy Marsden and her approach to keep on stepping; that is what this specific challenge was for me. I learned so much about my ability to undertake endurance challenges and the mental stamina entailed, and this gave me insights into my personal approach to business and life in general.

It's also about finding the resolve to keep on going when every step is painful and there is no compelling reason making you do this aside from some twisted sense of pride in getting to the finish line. There is always an easier option, which can and does include quitting. However, the stories, the insights, the camaraderie, the sense of achievement and the experiences would all be lost if I did that. I choose to step up physically and gain so much in my world of self-care by doing so; you are different to me, so choose a way in which this approach or thinking can be translated for you.

Create a regime that works for you

For some people the idea of creating a fitness regime sounds terrible. I have good news! Any regime, be that fitness, movement, nutrition or learning something new becomes easier if you take it one step at a time.

During the first lockdown in 2020, I set myself the simple challenge of 100 skips a day. In week two that went up to 200, and onwards up to week ten, when I hit 1,000 skips a day. At the beginning the maximum I could do in a row was four! Setting myself a daily challenge meant I couldn't miss a day. If I did, I had to do double the skips the following day.

I shared this challenge within my golfing community and enrolled approximately 50 others, all ranging in age, ability and fitness. Most of us were not skipping masters. It was a relatively simple challenge to complete, and during the 10 weeks a sense of pride emerged. I had never skipped as a child, and now I can.

As the number of daily skips grew, I shared some observations to help those taking part. The counting often went wrong as I got distracted or just tuned out – was it 42 or 52 skips in a row? Where am I up to now? Counting in bite-sized chunks or sets of 20s or 50s meant I only had to do a smaller number of sets and it was easier to keep track. Another option was to work out how many skips on average I did in a minute; it could be 25, 50, 100, so I was able to do the appropriate number of minutes to achieve the daily goal, plus a bit extra for good measure!

A priority before doing any exercise, no matter what age you are, is to stretch and warm up and then remember to stretch and warm down afterwards. Nobody wants any niggles and pulls from doing a challenge. If exercise is something you haven't done for a long time or you have other health issues, it would also be worth checking with your doctor before launching into something new.

Another consideration is what time of day is best for you. Some people are better first thing in the morning, before breakfast, to give the day a kick-start. Others need a mid-morning energy boost or want to shake out the morning Zoom calls before lunch. Or maybe mid-afternoon suits, when that siesta feeling beckons and you want to get yourself up and running again.

There isn't a right or wrong way, so do whatever works for you. Keeping to a semi-regular time slot worked best for me.

These techniques can be used in all areas of our lives, not just for skipping. Where else can you use them? As each new month arrives, you could choose a new challenge for the new month ahead. Here are some other options:

Chin-ups or squats: Whatever your maximum is in week one, be that two, three or 17, in the following week you must do one more than your previous maximum. Set it as a ten-week challenge or build it into your natural working day and target 50 in a row. That may sound impossible on day one but it really works.

Press-ups: Do one more press-up than you did the day before, for a month. You might start on 15, 45 or 100 as your day one maximum. Every day, increase by one, and at the end of each week on day 7, 14, 21, 28, go for it – how high can you get? Now set that higher total as your new base for the following week.

The 30-day plank challenge: Strengthen your core and build up endurance. Each day of the challenge, you'll gradually increase the amount of time that you hold a plank. At the end of the 30 days, the goal is to maintain a plank for 5 minutes straight. The 30-day plan:

1 20 secs	**2** 20 secs	**3** 30 secs	**4** 30 secs	**5** 40 secs	**6** rest
7 45 secs	**8** 45 secs	**9** 1 min	**10** 1 min	**11** 1 min	**12** 1½ mins
13 rest	**14** 1½ mins	**15** 1½ mins	**16** 2 mins	**17** 2 mins	**18** 2½ mins
19 rest	**20** 2½ mins	**21** 2½ mins	**22** 3 mins	**23** 3 mins	**24** 3½ mins
25 3½ mins	**26** rest	**27** 4 mins	**28** 4 mins	**29** 4½ mins	**30** 5 mins

If these fitness challenges don't work for you then choose a challenge that you can emotionally connect with. It can be anything from increasing your daily walk, riding your bike or learning to swim. See what inspiration you can unlock. Set a routine that will help you achieve the goal of improving and fine-tuning your physical wellbeing so you are able to take care of yourself as a whole. As strange as it may sound, I can vouch for the fact that a daily ritual of hundreds of skips can have a positive impact, both physically and mentally.

Clean up your nutrition

Do you remember the jingle for Mars Bars – 'Work, rest and play'? Nowadays, so many of us work a lot, rest a little and don't manage to play enough. We can achieve so much more when we have a fit body and mind. Yet it is hard to access all the necessary knowledge in the ever-evolving world of health, nutrition and fitness. Do you need a personal trainer, nutritionist, yoga sensei, mindfulness, strength and conditioning coach, physiotherapist, psychologist or simply a garden with a view?

For more than 20 years, I've stopped drinking alcohol every January. It all stems from needing a month off from drinking beer while playing competitive rugby. Over the years this developed from just excluding beer to being completely alcohol free, meat free, bread free, dairy free, sugar free and caffeine free. Wow, that's a lot when you type it out in black and white.

Being pure all the time is not my objective; it's about taking back control. I tend to lose a lot of weight doing this every year, but it's my personal performance levels where I really notice the difference. Of course, like many others undertaking a detox, during the first week there are headaches from sugar and caffeine withdrawal. Then it moves on to the need to graze a lot, and gradually the energy rebuilds, the brain fog of Christmas starts to clear, and overall there is a far bigger skip in my step.

The natural question is: why don't I live like this all of the time if it suits my body and energy levels? Well, to be honest, the other stuff is fun and very, very tasty. They always say have everything in moderation and you'll live longer. Well, that sounds great; I do like to party, I do like to play, and why not? Life is too short not to enjoy it.

My challenge to you is to have a go at cleaning things up if you need to. Take expert nutritional advice to increase your knowledge and help you plan what you want to achieve. Here is an evil question: 'Are you the heaviest you've ever been in your life at the moment?' Most of the people I've asked that question have answered yes (bearing in mind, for some, weight gain is the goal to becoming more healthy).

Weight isn't everything of course but society likes to impose ideal weights on each of us. Don't get me started on BMI! According to mine, I am obese and on the cusp of morbidly obese, purely because of my height-to-weight ratio. I have never met a rugby player (a forward) who isn't in the same boat; it's a calculation that doesn't show the accurate picture and is often incorrectly applied.

There is a great photo showing eight women of various sizes, shapes and heights, and they all weigh the same; the number on their scale could have a completely different meaning for each of them. Everyone has their own reasonable weight range – you know what that is for you and that is all you need to know, not what other uninformed people think is correct for you.

Try doing a run or swim with a 7 kg (1 st) bag strapped to your back for fun. It hurts, and you wouldn't choose to do it. When you are heavier you have indirectly chosen to carry that 7 kg bag under your skin. By cleaning the body of all the unhealthy stuff, exercise starts to pay dividends: the mind will follow.

My coach challenges me to be the best I can be every day of my life. My target is to be the best I can be most of the time, avoiding the trap of perfectionism. Strive for a fit body and mind. Who knows what more you could achieve? Remember, if you can't do it on your own, introduce the right support person to your self-care team.

Any fitness or healthcare regime will vary throughout your life. The workout that worked for you at the age of 21 will have changed by the time you are 22, let alone 42 or 53. Herein lies the problem: nobody but you knows that the equation is changing or has changed until you notice a difference. You can choose to do something about it before it affects your performance.

Different food types have a direct impact on me. I know that when I eat more oily fish and white meat with less bread and red meat, my brain fires far faster, I have clarity of vision and loads more energy and drive. Age can cause changes; foods you've never had a problem with before can start to affect you differently, and you're not sure why. Investigate this by keeping a food diary, in order to understand the changes in your performance and levels of fatigue. It can be enlightening and frightening.

Balance for you might include supplements, smoothies, juice bursts; the list goes on. Some are great and some not. Work out which ones suit you and enjoy them. I've tried various products, given up on many, and have an equation that works for me at the moment. I'm not trying to become the next Olympic gold medallist; I'm trying to be the best that I can be in all areas of my life.

It is the cumulative effect of sticking to a daily exercise and nutritional regime that changes the way your body works, and if you miss a day then you need to catch up. It's possible to cheat the system, but why would you when this is purely personal, and the benefits are all yours, meaning you would only be cheating yourself? Stick to it and reap the rewards.

Your body: summary

Not all approaches to your body and physical care involve extreme activities and big challenges: walking around the block, eating fewer takeaways and preparing your own meals are all methods that nutritionists and physical training instructors would advocate.

When I have been looking after the physical side of my self-care with diet and exercise, my brain fires faster, my stamina for work is increased and I can and do achieve far more. Knowing this, I would never attend an important business meeting, conference speech or sales pitch having been out drinking and playing the night before. That's not just about respect for the client, my reputation and not wanting to smell of alcohol or look tired; it's about keeping my brain sharp and being able to give the best performance I can without sabotaging my performance.

Translate these elements of setting personal challenges, consistent stepping, regime development and looking after your nutrition so they make sense for you, and recruit the relevant people into your support team that will help you along this path. Your challenges will be very different to mine; they are personal to you and will motivate you to get on with whatever it takes to become successful. Are your physical self-care challenges big enough to get you committed to seeing them through? If they seem too big today, who can you enrol to help you along the way?

Reboot and rebuild

Everyone needs downtime. Some might call it escapism, others call it mindfulness or meditation. It can be whatever works for you. There is so much going on in our heads, both consciously and unconsciously; it is possible to manage that inner noise, refocus the chatter and create calm.

The place where I go to reboot or reinvigorate has always been sport. It's almost like a religion to me, as I contemplate it daily – from my days playing rugby for a premiership club through to trying to stay alive in a water polo pool.

Sport has always allowed me to release my anger and angst. It's my zen place – it gives me focus, hunger and passion as well as being a form of meditation. I'm good, but not good enough to make a living from it – although I'm good enough to make an impact as part of a team. Where is your zen place?

You need balance between your dedication and taking time to relax and reflect. Meditation could be an ideal way to help you 'switch off the noise'. Trial and error is required to find what works for you. For many years I've accepted that meditation could help me, but had chosen to avoid it as I considered it a bit flaky; I didn't understand its benefits and never managed to clear my head. No disrespect to those that practise it; it just hasn't been on my radar. Trying to ignore the head chatter without assistance hasn't worked and I now practise meditation, albeit irregularly, with some noticeable benefits.

Whether you download a meditation app or simply do a search on YouTube, you can easily find guided or unguided meditation sessions of varying lengths. My initial fear was that every time I sat with my eyes shut I would fall asleep, but I have to say that doesn't happen very often. Now I can honestly say that after just five minutes of meditation, I feel fresher and more alert.

Finding the time is the standard excuse, daily, weekly or annually. Every year we get several bank holidays; what does a bank holiday mean to you? An extra day off work? Chores, chores and more chores that you have been putting off for months and from which there is now no escape? Or time for you to reboot and rebuild? Whatever a bank holiday means to you there aren't many of them, so why would you choose to waste them?

Giving yourself time for recovery, rebooting and reflecting is very different from doing nothing and just losing a day. How often do you visit a massage therapist, have a manicure or attend a wine tasting? These are all activities that can help you reboot and rebuild. What works for you?

I'm not the most gifted at DIY; it's not my strength. I give it a go and generally end up hiring a professional to finish off (or make good) what I have done. On a bank holiday DIY would not be my first choice of activity.

For me, my choices will range from a round of golf to climbing a mountain or swimming in a lake on my own or with some of my family in tow. Of course, that's just me! A trip to a country house, the theatre, visiting friends or building something works just as well.

It's your turn now. Plan how you will use your time during your bank holidays in the year ahead. These are bonus days, so make them count, make them special/different/memorable. You could even create a Bank Holiday Bucket List. Not everyone aspires to be a weekend warrior doing random extreme activities. What is your equivalent?

Even though we need others to help us achieve the right strategies and balance, self-care is your responsibility. Some of the people you need to help you reboot and rebuild will be personal to you. For example, I know that my wife's fear of the dentist is quite extreme, and when the holidays come around and the dentist closes, there will always be a coincidental dental challenge. To manage this situation and provide the necessary reassurance, she has his personal mobile number. I can't relate to this myself but for her it is so important.

Who do you need around you to help you reboot from the day-to-day demands of life – doctor, coffee-shop owner, neighbour, school friend, dentist, pub landlord, hairdresser, bank manager, therapist, sports teammates...? There are no right or wrong answers – your support network is relevant and real for you. Nobody else, just you, and that's OK.

The self-care checklist

Looking after ourselves is not being selfish – it will help us perform at our best more of the time. So much self-sabotage happens when we neglect the primary focus in our lives, which is looking after number one. Take the time to focus your self-care on your mind and body while factoring in that all-important time to reboot and rebuild along the way.

Ultimately everything is your choice. Remember that not taking action to improve your self-care is a choice to accept the status quo and remain where you are. A balance between your mind and body self-care regime is really important for your long-term success and prosperity. Surrounding yourself with Dynamos that motivate and stimulate your energy and Rocks who keep you grounded and on track can make all the difference. Use this list to prioritise and question how you plan to take care of yourself:

- How are you going to make sure you are number one?
- What are you going to do to improve your self-care?
- Who are you going to engage to help you?
- Do you know what fun looks like for you now?
- Who will teach you meditation?
- How will you improve your diet?
- How will you make yourself accountable to others?
- What community or tribe are you going to get involved with?
- How are you going to invest in developing positive mental health?
- How will you take responsibility for your successes and failures?
- How can you create an environment in which you can enjoy yourself?
- If your energy is off, can you work out why and make changes?

Finally, I wanted to mention two books that really touched my core when I read them: *Man's Search for Meaning* by Victor Frankl; and *The Choice* by Dr Edith Eger. Both books were written about surviving in Nazi concentration camps. Don't be put off by the grim nature of the subject matter. They will help you learn about strength, resilience and spiritual survival – all essential for self-care.

The Coach

Coaching is not about teaching and telling; it's about discovery and unlocking potential and success. As a result of working with a coach, you take action. Only you are responsible for your progress – your inaction is not the coach's fault.

Coaches come in many guises, from being a role model within your circle of family and friends, to a sports team coach, through to a professional coach that you engage for your business. Coaching relationships are built on a foundation of great questions, actions and accountability, focused on finding the best way for an individual to achieve their goals.

Before coaching can begin, a chemistry check is required to establish if there is a good connection between the coach and the person wanting to be coached, and success is therefore likely. Questions that regularly come up are 'Can you afford a coach?' versus 'Can you afford not to have a coach?' That is a decision for you to make.

Not all coaching is expensive; there are many organisations that provide coaching services supported by government finance or within educational establishments. Another way is via the accreditation bodies (such as the Association for Coaches or the International Coach Federation), which require trainee coaches to rack up pro bono coaching hours in order to qualify. However, a serious point to note is that, whether you are paying or not, coaching can become an expensive fireside chat if you do nothing as a result of your sessions.

To get you started, here's a quick summary of my top ten benefits of having a coach:

- continual one-on-one attention to what's important
- personal accountability for development, direction and self-improvement
- increased self-awareness of blind spots and unconscious habits and practice

- learning and support when the situation or circumstances require external input
- a professional confidante with a curious and collaborative focus on your best interests
- someone to get you out of your comfort zone because they believe in your potential and will expand your thinking
- someone to help you find the right way for you to go around, through or over obstacles that limit your success
- more job and life satisfaction
- more effective contribution to a team and an organisation
- more effective and productive communication.

Before deciding if you need a coach, let's set some context and ground rules for a coaching relationship and what sort of coach you might require.

A coach does not need to be an expert in the area you specialise in, but they do need to be able to empower and assist you in uncovering your secret formula for success. A coach will help you discover the areas that are holding you back and agree on the steps to take to see an action through to completion.

A coach does not dictate what to do, as might happen in a parent or employee type situation. They are trying to help you access your emotional connection to the desired result. Unlocking the emotional connection between where you are now and what you want to achieve is the foundation of all behavioural change. Without such a connection, behavioural change will not occur. An emotional connection can be to the vision of yourself on a beach in that swimsuit with all your lumps and bumps receiving compliments from passers-by; giving up smoking; or simply not leading a lifestyle that means you might die before you get to meet your grandchildren. When the emotional connection is big enough and personal enough to you, the necessary behavioural change will follow.

Which coach is best for you when there are so many to choose from?

- **personal training coach – to get you over that next threshold or under that time**

- **business and performance coach – for business interests, growth and global domination**

- **life coach – to help you unlock your true calling in life and the direction you should follow**

- **speaking and confidence coach – for making you memorable when you stand up and present**

- **relationship coach – for those all-important personal goals and obstacles.**

Then there are also coaches for sales, dancing, swimming, language, managing teenagers, grief, alcohol – the list goes on.

You now move into the world of trial and error as you discover which coach is correct for you and for the task at hand. Yes, you can have more than one coach for different parts of your life and career; the issue can be conflicting ideas and direction, so tread carefully. Also, many coaches will have more than one area of focus and their title can be misleading.

I am known as a performance and business coach helping clients to raise the bar of their success levels and achieve more than they would on their own. In addition I regularly work with individuals on areas that affect their fitness, mental health and even nutrition. While these are not my specialist areas of expertise, I can stimulate a great deal of insight and debate, and give direction for further analysis.

Coaching is not to be confused with mentoring, consulting, therapy or counselling. Here is my simple guide, designed to get you thinking.

What does a coach do? I work in the world of applied coaching and start with a blank piece of paper. I do not turn up with a pharmacy full of solutions looking to prescribe various remedies for the client. The objective is to help the individual find their own path, their own motivation and direction, in an environment where a commitment to action is made. It's their action, their process and their goal – nobody else's. Because of this fact alone the probability of seeing this action through to the end is far greater because they own it.

What is a mentor? A mentor shares stories, experience and personally earned wisdom. The skill of the mentor is to share their knowledge and inspire the mentee to take action and learn without having to go through all that experience themselves.

What is a consultant? A consultant provides independent analysis of a situation or challenge through the eyes of an external individual or a team. They assess, investigate and then come back with a report, method or solution to fix the issue. In many cases their engagement ends with the handover of the report; however, they may go on to implement their findings or launch the new processes and systems. The client in this situation can be one step away from the learning at all times and will gain less knowledge and wisdom through the experience because they are not the person applying it. Hence when, or if, the solution should fail, the consultant gets the blame and their contract is terminated.

What is a counsellor? In counselling an individual is encouraged to talk about their feelings and emotions with a qualified counsellor who'll listen to and support them in a non-judgemental way without criticising or challenging them.

What is a therapist? A therapist helps an individual gain a better understanding of their feelings and thought processes, and helps them find solutions to psychological and emotional problems. They do not give advice or tell someone what to do.

In my work I fluctuate between all five skill sets at different times according to what is necessary in that moment. There are many occasions where a more directive approach is needed versus a more quiet, listening, supportive ear.

As do all good coaches, I know my limitations and introduce qualified therapists if the client is becoming more of a patient and in need of specific support. A skilled coach will share wisdom, knowledge and analysis while empowering the client to take ownership of the way ahead.

It would be unwise of me not to touch on how these services are paid for; clearly, support like this has a cost attached to it as would be expected with any professional service. Fees will vary wildly between a coach working at an executive corporate level, a role model sharing some ideas and thoughts or a counsellor based within a charity.

Having a coach in your corner

Problems and opportunities are often said to be the same things depending on what lens you are looking through, whether it's your vision or someone else's point of view. How does this relate to your business approach? Do you have one or two people that you can bounce ideas off and help you formulate your plans?

A coach will help you to knuckle down to your priorities, put a line through multiple items on the to-do list, ask quality questions and evaluate various options on the dashboard. These actions will cumulatively build momentum, with growing evidence that your efforts are worthwhile.

Forget about looking at a long list of activities; just focus on a small number of priorities at any one time. With your coach's support, you can put together a shortlist of quantifiable action points.

Successful coaching relies on total honesty and vulnerability. It will be obvious if you do not complete the actions you have committed to or manipulate statistics to make you sound and feel better. With a good coach, you should not be able to get away with it – they will see right through you!

A previous coach of mine shared a simple life formula that I subscribe to wholeheartedly:

Performance = Potential – Interference

Performance: How do you define positive performance? What criteria do you use to measure your service? Is it quantifiable, qualitative or spiritual? There are so many different measurable criteria. You choose.

Potential: This word has so many challenges attached to it. If you are anything like me, your school report consistently stated 'could do better' or 'if he put 10% of the effort into his work that he does on the rugby pitch he could be a genius'. Our full potential is something that is often seen by others and not by ourselves, and when we do happen to see it, we tend to discount it or disbelieve it.

Interference: This is quite simply everything that goes on inside our minds and all around us that distracts and pollutes the potential we have. Everything I just described about my school report was interference in one form or another. We self-sabotage and prevent ourselves from being the best we can be most of the time.

On a couple of business trips – one an association convention, the other a week's intensive learning towards my Advanced Accreditation in Executive Coaching – my head space was very different from normal. On both occasions, I was mentally and physically away from everything else going on in my world, and time zones prevented ease of communication with family and clients alike. The intensity of the situation prevented me from accessing (with ease) email and social media. I was in Mikey's Bubble, free from distraction.

During that time, my mind was so sharp, so switched on and so alert to everything going on around me, absorbing and appreciating the learning, both personally and professionally. I am not suggesting we all need to run away to the mountains, but if that works for you, do it.

You need to find the environment, with a coaching catalyst behind you, where you can truly switch off all the interference that goes on every day, and focus on allowing your full potential to shine through. It does none of us any favours achieving 50% or 72% of our full potential. The person that loses out here is you and potentially your family and loved ones. What is getting in the way of you going into your performance bubble more of the time?

What does this have to do with having a coach, I hear you ask? The challenge, I believe, is to find the lifestyle that is right for each of us; after all, hard drugs and rock 'n' roll is not the calling for most. At times you may feel blocked by a wall of fear, doubt or negative self-belief that prevents you from trying. A coach will help you experiment with different approaches and hopefully uncover your burning desire for success.

Remember you are alive!

What does the definition of 'living' mean to you? When do you hope to feel truly alive again? Put that plan in place with your coach, family or significant other and move from purely existing to LIVING!

We all want to experience that feeling of being glad to be alive! However, during the course of our lives, we can learn new fears; for example, I never used to have a fear of heights. It has developed since having children, getting into situations where they would wander off oblivious to the massive drop down the stairs or over a balcony.

For me, attempting to climb Mont Blanc brought home the fact that I am not comfortable with heights. During the training, in order to overcome that fear, our team took on mentors and coaches; we trusted expert guides, their advice, skills and knowledge, to keep us alive while climbing this awesome peak.

On day one we did a colossal 50m ice-wall climb, trudged up and down glaciers and waded through waist-high deep snow, things that I could never have done without their guidance and the belief that we were safe in their keeping.

After three days of training and learning, our guides informed us that we would not be able to attempt to summit Mont Blanc because of the amount of snow that had fallen. The risk of avalanches was too high, so, unfortunately, we had to climb elsewhere. Our new target was Aiguille du Tour, a longer climb with a pinnacle summit, almost as tall as Mont Blanc. The goal changed in an instant because of our instructors' experience and respect for Mother Nature. We were disappointed but listened to their advice.

Three weeks later, after Mont Blanc had said no to us, nine climbers were killed by an unexpected avalanche in the exact place where we would have been. The teams included some very experienced climbers, along with have-a-go novice climbers like ourselves.

It wasn't our time. Others have said that we were lucky. I am certainly glad to be alive. It is sobering when an event such as this occurs, and I am thankful to the guides who steered us away from a dangerous situation.

This close call reminds me of another one. The rugby club I played for while living in Perth, Australia would go on some truly beautiful rugby tours, including Bali. We decided not to go one year. Sadly (and fortunately for us) that was the year of the Bali bombing, and many of the players involved in the tournament were caught up in the tragedy. Luck or serendipity? I don't know, but it's very humbling.

I do believe in *carpe diem* – seize the day. I am focused on not wasting a single precious moment. Those instructors in the mountains were our coaches at that time and worked with us on the risk analysis and then created a new plan that we went on to achieve. I avoided these two disasters by a stroke of luck in the one case and professional insight and judgement on the other. Having the confidence and belief in the support network around you can make so much difference and could potentially, in some instances, save your life

Ask yourself this question: what have you done, achieved or experienced recently? So many of these happy and positive memories take place every day of our lives, and we can be guilty of taking them for granted when they deserve to be remembered and given greater focus.

When I eventually go, I do not want it to be said that I didn't try, that I sat back and watched, that I was a spectator rather than a player, or that I could have achieved so much more. All of these phrases send shivers down my spine. I need to believe that I have given everything my best shot, had a go and played full out; and yet I know there are times when I fail to achieve this. Having a coach, helping me to achieve more than I would on my own, is essential for my success – unlocking those marginal gains and dispelling those imposter fears and doubts that we all have.

We have all lost family, friends, relations, parents and close mates far too early, like my friend Tom. I believe they all had more to give. What could a coach or a mental wealth team have unlocked or discovered had they been involved?

Looking from the outside in

There are times when we all need an external view in order to really understand what's going on. You may be very good at long-term endurance planning and training, but most people struggle to create these plans and can often lose sight of the big picture. Another point of view can uncover many seemingly obvious errors or different approaches that could really aid your progress and direction.

A very clear example of this is the wonderful team of proofreaders that worked on this book. As do most authors, I became extremely word blind, and having different people asking questions about my intent or direction enabled me to crystallise my points and find flow for each paragraph and chapter.

The external view of your world through a different lens can be so insightful. Here's what my speaking friend Roger Harrop – known pro-fessionally as 'The Man in the Helicopter' – shared with me.

I'm telling all business leaders around the world the same thing. These days, more than ever before, you've got to spend at least 20% of your time 'in the helicopter' looking at the big picture of yourself and your business. That's one day a week. But to get in that helicopter you've got to get good at talking to yourself – and listening!

Business is really simple – it's us that makes it complicated. Someone has something to buy, someone has something to sell, and maybe someone has to make something – that's all it is!

From your helicopter you've first got to be crystal-clear where it is you're trying to get to – what's your purpose, why does the business exist and why are you running it? If you don't know where it is you're trying to get to, how do you stand any chance of getting there?

I once ran a masterclass for a group of 15 CEOs – various business sectors, various sizes, some owner CEOs, some 'hired hands'.

We got to the end of the morning and the chair said to one of the CEOs: 'Norman, we seemed to lose you earlier – why?' Norman responded with: 'Yes, you're right – what Roger was saying struck a chord with me. As you know I've been running our third-generation toy business for three years, and I'm sick of it. We're getting nowhere. My father interferes, my aunt and other family members tell people what to do and we have no idea where we are going. We have a family board meeting tomorrow and I've decided to tear up the agenda and replace it with one item – purpose – and it's going to be like electing the Pope – we're going to sit there until the smoke comes out of the chimney!'

He rang me later in the week and told me how it went. He said: 'It was absolute hell – but we got there. We have all agreed on our purpose and our commitment to getting there. And do you know what? I felt the stress instantly fall off my shoulders.'

So how do you find that elusive 20% of your time? You have to trust people more and delegate. No matter how young or experienced they are, don't micromanage them.

Don't let yourself get sucked into the mud and bullets. If you have a task to be done, give it to the team, tell them to evaluate and come up with proposed action and alternatives but at a certain time, and then stand back and observe. You will be amazed by what you see and the clarity it gives you.

Following this advice, you need to make time to look down on your activities – but how? How can you switch off that noise and clear your head? How can you possibly take time out when there is so much going on? Maybe you think nobody understands the business as well as you do, and wonder how it will cope in your absence.

Nowadays, everything seems to require an immediate response and switching off completely, even for a short time, can be a challenge. Looking from the outside in can give you the ability to evaluate and assess what is important. That is where the power of an external viewpoint – the coach – really comes to the fore, speaking the unspoken and asking the previously avoided or ignored questions! Now is the time to develop some new habits and give you the kick-start you need.

Building new habits

A habit is a regular action or activity that can be good or bad. In many cases, once a habit has taken root, it's something that you do regularly, without being aware you are doing it. These behaviours become ingrained in your everyday routines and can become very difficult to break.

Engaging a buddy partner or coach will dramatically increase your chances of creating or breaking a habit. By giving these people permission to give you a hard time if you fail to stick to your target, you are far more likely to be successful more quickly than on your own.

In business, as in life, you can spend ages deliberating how to break these old habits – the ones that keep you busy, make you unhealthy or prevent your brilliance from shining. So maybe it's time to build some new habits.

Creating a new habit and committing to it for the rest of your life is just too big a goal and is likely to fail. Commit to just 30 days. That's all: 30 days of doing whatever it is that you want to do differently.

Much research has been done into how long it takes to create a new habit – some researchers say 21 days, others 18, 66 or even 256. It depends on the size of the habit and how different it is to the standard way of working. Doing the new habit for 30 days will give you a great start, and that then becomes another 30 days, and so on.

My friend the neuroscientist Dr Lynda Shaw avoids all subjective numerical targets around days or attempts when creating a new habit.

She is adamant that replacing an existing habit requires something more attractive, more fun, or has a higher value to it. This is because if the new behaviour is rewarding, we are more likely to repeat it, thus making it a habit. The process can be instant or take an extended amount of time; it's down to the individual and the environment.

Aim for excellence, not perfection. Avoid any form of black and white sum where failure is an option; progress is the target. I'm not talking about changing an addictive habit such as giving up smoking or drinking. The focus here is on creating a new habit, meaning you can be imperfect and run it as an experiment.

For example, many people I know have step counters and are adopting the activity target of 10,000 steps per day. Aiming for perfection can lead some people to walking the streets at 10pm trying to hit that daily goal.

Let's look at this more constructively and allow imperfection. Out of the 30 days available in a month, you successfully achieve your target 25 times; that's a success rate of more than 80%, which is not a bad start. Clearly, on those days when you miss the target, you are aware of what you have achieved, be that 3,000 or 6,000 steps, which will all contribute to your daily average for the month.

Part of the process is creating a constructive habit loop – routine, reward, cue/trigger. Build the routine and maybe add in a conservative reward (not always food- or drink-related). The challenge is to find your cue or trigger. What starts you off on this new habit? Can you create a morning ritual where before you can do Y you must do X?

It reminds me of when I was a child and I ate all the 'ugly' vegetables before I could enjoy the good stuff!

Choose a translation of this that resonates with you. Everything is just a theory until you make it real. Simple examples for me would include cold calling, or completing my tax returns and annual accounts. Each of these tasks needs to be completed, and creating a reward system for myself prevents me from procrastinating and faffing about.

To consolidate a new habit requires the removal of excessive options and temptations; if you have a shopping list full of possibilities on day one, the chances are you will fail. I refer back to Joy Marsden's words again here and *keep on stepping* – taking small steps forward at a time without stopping. By only having a couple of options on the go at one time, your new habit is far more likely to take root and become an established way of working. Replacing old habits with new, improved and more fun ones makes it so much easier to break unhelpful patterns.

A technique that I use every year is to visualise the positive feeling of achievement that I would like to experience at the end of the year. I know I can only achieve this through long-term small steps, training or action. For example, at Christmas, having completed what you were visualising, how might it feel to be sitting at the table with a massive smile on your face because you have succeeded with your goal or established that new habit?

The Christmas after I swam the English Channel, each member of our team was banned from wearing Christmas party hats. We had to wear swim hats to our Christmas meal. Gordon was in a posh restaurant with his special lady, I was in my family dining room, Charlie was at his in-laws': we all looked ridiculous and it felt really good!

Every year my family is set a reflective challenge. We all look at the three things we are proud to have achieved that year and set three things that we aim to have completed by the same time the following year. Simple goal-setting, I hear you say. Correct! Everyone now has 365 days to develop and implement the necessary habits. With the aid of your coach, you too can make this happen; wishful thinking doesn't work.

Help comes from asking better questions

Coaches ask questions. You need to be clear and precise about the help you require from your coach. Relying on someone else's sixth sense does not work; unfortunately a telepathy app hasn't yet been invented. You must trust someone enough to ask for help, and be honest and direct in your requests.

My coaching has taken me into many different areas. I've worked with CEOs of entrepreneurial businesses, sporting heroes transitioning into new careers, and even unmotivated teenagers. I've also been involved in the world of mental health and wellbeing. I'm all too aware that asking better questions is vital to uncovering the truth of a situation.

I have seen teenagers who feel it's uncool to show signs of weakness that can be exploited or picked upon; a footballer who avoided seeking out the best player to ask for advice on a particular move due to the fear of rejection; and a leader, isolated at the top of their company, haunted by their responsibilities to their family, their employees and the business.

Each of these scenarios can have a massive impact on self-esteem and self-belief, sowing the seed for deeper issues in the future, including clinical diagnosis. One of the biggest challenges is creating an environment that encourages people to ask for help.

All coaches have their own style. This emphasises the importance of the initial chemistry check to make sure the coach and coachee are right for each other. Direct language and questioning can appear harsh to an individual who finds it hard to imagine a better future and is suffering from mental health issues. There are many ways to ask the same question without losing the potency or potential to unlock the necessary answers. Great coaches have the ability to adapt their style and approach to the coachee.

Here are some questions that a coach could ask. I have asked them many times. Some will make you think, squirm and reflect, whereas others will seem less relevant to you at this point in time.

- Where will you be in a year or five years from now if things don't change?

- What is within your control to create, change or influence?

- When you listen to your thoughts and that little voice in your head, how are you using your energy?

- If you could change anything, what would it be?

- What will it take to shift your thoughts and actions to focus more on what is within your control?

- What do you wish was different?

- How often do you think about things that could go wrong?

- When you're not busy/when you're lying in bed at night, what are the things that make you feel the most upset?

- What do you wish you could change about yourself in all of this?

♟ What do you think might go wrong here?

♟ What's the most frustrating part of everything that is going on?

♟ What is going on for you that doesn't help?

♟ What helps you cope?

♟ Do you know why you are so upset about what's going on?

♟ What would be one step forward you could take?

It's up to you how you process the answers. Have any of them made you feel uncomfortable? Uncomfortable enough for you to want to take action? If so, what are you going to do? Taking no action is always an option, but that will mean nothing changes. If it was just a random list of questions that meant nothing to you today, that's OK as well. The questions will percolate in the back of your mind and when, or if, one becomes relevant you will consider it further.

Better questions create conversations, discussions and insights that can really make a difference to your understanding of what is either holding you back or where the potential opportunities exist that you haven't thought of before.

Total immersion and big, fat, hairy goals

Let's get your mindset positioned correctly for a professional approach to life. We can all be guilty of dabbling in something rather than playing full out, so a coach will help you to raise your game. How often, if you are truly honest, do you go out with the brakes still on, preventing you from going at full speed?

One of the best ways to learn something new or take on a new challenge is through total immersion. Go and live in the country to learn the language, or go on a yoga retreat where workshops are taking place five times a day. Jumping in will fast-track your learning and deliver a real transformation in a relatively short amount of time. You will also meet like-minded souls who will give you positive energy and great stories about their own life journeys to that point.

I once attended an improvisation skills retreat delivered by some of the best instructors and coaches in the industry. Some of the other participants had been on stages around the world as improv artists and performers, whereas I was a total newbie with zero experience.

There were five days of classes, morning, noon and night, teaching techniques, processes and singing. Yes, I ended up singing to a room full of strangers, making up lyrics off the cuff. It was such a stretch and seriously good fun as well. Fully immersing myself in the environment, coaching, mentoring and development meant that my learning and understanding grew quickly and dramatically.

So what are you claiming to be fully committed to, but in reality you are only dabbling in as if it were a hobby? What steps could you take for total immersion that would have a positive and potentially enormous impact? Real commitment creates real change; it's time to create space in your diary so you can take control and choose who will help you get there.

As I said before, behavioural change will only happen if there is an emotional connection to the outcome. You must connect to the goal, otherwise you won't care enough and probably won't be motivated enough to achieve it.

David Hyner, a brilliant motivational speaker and facilitator who talks about setting 'massive goals', is a great pal of mine. I asked him for a quote about goal-setting – and he didn't hold back.

> At the time of writing, I have spent my spare time researching and interviewing 258 top achievers to establish how they set and go about achieving their goals. Guess how many of them, when asked the question 'How do you set goals?' answered by saying either 'SMART* goals', or 'realistic and achievable'?
>
> ZERO, none, zilch, zip, nada, nil.... Not one of them!? So why are we so taken in, and convinced, by people who tell us to set realistic goals?
>
> Do yourself a favour and the next time somebody asks you to set a SMART or realistic goal, ask them, 'What is that based on?' Nobody has been able to answer that for me, including business schools and top-flight advisers who preach the SMART goal gospel.
>
> The guy who invented the SMART theory was George T. Doran. A very nice man, and a project manager who worked on HUGE

water utility projects. He set MASSIVE goals but 'actioned' smart steps towards the larger goal.

In my opinion, he has been massively misquoted! Do yourself a favour and set yourself (to quote Tim Watts, the founder of Pertemps recruitment) a BIG, FAT, HAIRY GOAL!

(*SMART stands for Specific, Measurable, Achievable, Relevant and Time-bound.)

Can you honestly achieve your definition of success on your own? Are your goals big enough, consistent with where you want to head, or do you resist setting goals? A coach will ask you these questions consistently and reflect on where you are making progress and staying motivated. Nobody feels motivated all the time; the wheels will and do come off. It doesn't mean that you are a failure (or any other ugly things that you might say to yourself), so get back up, reach out for support and move forward – that's the whole point of building your mental wealth team.

In the mid-1990s the sport of rugby union switched from being an amateur sport to professional. However, for many years the top players did make money, but it wasn't money going into the bank. In rugby, it was known as 'boot money'. After playing a game, there was an envelope of cash placed inside your boot while you were in the shower or bath. Yes, I am old enough to remember communal muddy baths after matches!

The general understanding is that as a 'professional' you receive payment for what you do. Yet there are many people in business, sport, the charitable sector or education who receive payment for what they do but are far from professional in their approach, activities or delivery.

What then does it take to be professional in business and life in general? Striving to be the best version of yourself would be a reasonable description; however, these are just words. A coach helps you consistently perform at your best most of the time. That is the art of being a professional – being coached and challenged along the way, so you are fit for purpose physically and mentally for the road ahead.

A professional mindset means always striving to be the best, taking personal responsibility to research and prepare for every eventuality. Professionals do not leave things to chance; amateurs hope for the best and try not to screw it up when they get there. There are many times when we have all winged it and succeeded despite our amateur approach. But what has that approach cost us in lost prospects and squandered opportunities? The professional approach means having a coach on your mental wealth team to keep you immersed in all your goals; the bigger, fatter and hairier, the better.

The coach checklist

I have asked myself every single question on this list multiple times throughout my life. Sometimes I like the answers I get and others I don't, and so I take steps to change the situation. Some questions will resonate more with you than others; that's the point, we can't change, fix or adapt everything all at one time. If you want a coach, ask these questions of yourself to determine what and who you need:

- What type of coach do you need? Personal, life, business? Specific? Ask around, ask your network, ask your mental wealth team.

- How much time can you allocate to a coach?

- What is your budget? Large or small?

- Is it short term or potentially long term?

- Do you want a pedant or the relaxed approach?

- Are you open to sharing and being honest?

- Who do you already know that you've met at networking meetings? Were you intrigued? Could you work with them? Follow up with a coffee.

- Does the chemistry feel right? Are you happy going on a journey of investigation and discovery with this person?

- If you're a good match, then engage and away you go, always with clear objectives.

- Set regular reviews of progress to make sure it works for you.

The Professional Support Team

Back in the old days, the key person in your professional support team would have been your bank manager. They knew everyone, had a significant number of products on offer and would always aim to find a solution that was right for you. They were always proactive, supportive and made time for you. But those days have long gone; the focus is now on productivity and profit, as clearly demonstrated by the 2008 banking crisis, which deepened the gaping void of trust within the banking world. Now that you're less likely to have a special relationship with your bank manager, who could be on your professional support team?

During our lives, we go through many stages of transition – from child to student, employee, parent, entrepreneur, leader and eventually retiree. The trusted advisors we need support from will vary accordingly. I don't believe those in the professional support team need to be on speed dial and available 24/7; however, you need to know who they are and where they are so you can get hold of them if necessary. These are the people who understand what you are trying to achieve and where you are heading.

The critical question is: who *should* be on your professional team? Both my father and father-in-law passed on their advice to never work with family and friends, as it can ruin a relationship. However, my father's financial wealth and legal support were provided by his father's firm and later his brother when their father passed away. My father-in-law used his best friend's firm to provide similar services for all his support over many decades.

Fortunately, these professional relationships didn't go wrong for them, but could have, and they were willing to take that risk. Professional relationships require an intimate level of honesty, openness, vulnerability and understanding, built on a very close working relationship – and family and close friends have an inside track here.

There are three broad subdivisions of professional support: wealth management, legal and accountancy. Financial worries are one of the greatest and most frequent causes of mental stress, so planning to manage these pressures proactively will go a long way. Choosing the appropriate team members will help you to avoid financial misery and general angst.

Good-quality professional advice will cost good money. That's a key learning point. If you are paying for it, you are far more likely to listen, learn and act accordingly than if you just search for answers on Google.

There will always be unsolicited advice that comes from well-meaning friends, autocratic bosses, teachers and family members. You can choose to listen to the advice, assess it on its merits and relevance to you and then make your own decision.

Many entrepreneurs would probably not have achieved success had they waited for someone to come up with good advice, and wouldn't even have looked for it. These guys don't wait; they go for it. And yes, they screw up from time to time and choose to bounce back from failure, pick themselves up and start all over again.

Winging it is a risky way to run a business, yet people still do it. What risk do you run by taking shortcuts? Can you afford to take that risk? There aren't any risk-free shortcuts here; trying to play the system or break the rules is where you can get caught out.

One area that is never worth taking a risk over is reputation. Honesty and integrity are important qualities in business, and recovering from reputational challenges can be tough. An old adage that still holds true: it takes years to build a great relationship, and only seconds to completely break it. Breaking the law is obviously not acceptable. Nor is the excuse that 'it's just standard industry practice, everybody manipulates the figures and results'.

Shortcuts towards easy money or not doing due diligence may seem a good idea at the time, but will they be in the long run? Ask yourself these questions:

- What impact (both positive and negative) could this have on your reputation, professionally or personally?

- Where can you find the best advice to ensure your decisions do not leave you exposed or vulnerable to incompetence, fraud or criminal activity?

- Can you afford not to take this advice?

Remember that paid-for advice almost always works out cheaper in the long run. A professional support team will protect you from many of these sticky situations; however, mistakes can still occur. You can reduce the potential for negative fallout by seeking risk analysis and professional advice in the following areas: wealth manager, legal eagle, accountant. Your professional team may look different to these according to your industry, niche or location, so build the team that works for you.

The wealth manager

This is the member of your professional support team who aims to provide you with 'a plentiful supply of a particular desirable thing'. Many practitioners in the world of wealth management focus on creating the life you want through long-term financial management and investments. There are highs and lows as markets fluctuate and economies go in and out of recession, so short-term gains are not the objective here. You're looking for secure wealth for life.

The wealth manager looks after the bigger picture – where you are placing your money now and where it needs to be in the future. Whether you desire expensive cars, a property portfolio or a comfortable stress-free lifestyle, someone other than you needs to understand how you can make that possible.

Here's what my wealth manager, Bart Dalton, told me:

> That wealthy people are typically happier is partially true – they just have other problems. When someone becomes wealthy they decide that the level of money they currently possess can afford them the experiences, things and time that they have always desired, with some to spare just in case.

> It might seem that a successful person doesn't need a team. Look at Tiger Woods. He took on the PGA and the stigma of golf being a sport that was old, stale and pale. Michael Phelps became the most medalled Olympian ever because of his dedication to the pool. But behind Tiger and Michael there were droves of coaches, doctors, nutritionists, media specialists, accountants, lawyers and overall supporters. The same rings true when it comes to your success and applies to your wealth. You need to build a team that has the same goals in mind, i.e. yours.

Teams are composed of specialists focused on delivering to the best of their abilities to deliver a specific outcome. Your wealth is a goal that needs to be discussed, planned and delivered by a team of professionals that understand where they are all working to help you get to. Your team will include legal, tax and financial planners.

The missing ingredient is typically twofold. First, your specific vision of your direction of travel, and second, your permission to keep you in line with the targeted end goal. In my book *The Assisted Purchase*, I talk about the '3G advisor' whose goal is to be the Guru, Guide and Gladiator. Someone on your wealth team needs to be given the ultimate power to keep you corralled through tough times. The Gladiator is the most sparingly used, but most important of all of these players. They have your permission to tell you that you are going against all of your goals and might not meet them! They get to tell you to pull your socks up and get back on track.

The reason you need a team with your vision at its centre is that there are numerous routes to get to your destination, and most importantly everyone has an opinion of the best route to take. Your wealth team needs to keep this in mind, and if you don't want to be the only voice, one of your team needs to be the trusted advisor with the 3G powers bestowed by you to lead the team. Get your vision sorted with your team or at least the start of your team. Tiger had his swing coach, putting coach and legal team. Michael had his swim coach, nutritionist and medical team. So if these people at the top of their game needed a team to guide them to success, so do you.

When working with a wealth manager, total honesty is essential. Candid conversations about salaries and financial goals do not usually take place with members of your own family. Do you know your parents' salaries or income? This might make it less natural or uncomfortable to have revealing conversations with an outsider that you have appointed to your professional support team. Without transparency, it just doesn't work. An effective support team will know when you are holding back, so there's no need to hide behind a mask!

It's easy to see how hiding the truth can become a habit and the 'mask' becomes stuck; this is not sustainable. In my days in the corporate world, I felt that I was guided to hide my personality and became a bit of a robot. Don't show your humour or your passions; just do your job. So I wore a corporate mask and hid my individuality.

Now is the time to remove any mask and share uncomfortable truths with your team. We all know that people buy people. It's you that they connect with, it's you who stands out from the crowd as there is only one of you – so why hide your truth, your authenticity? How can an advisor help you if you wear a mask and don't share your truth with them?

When my parents died, my sister and I had an opportunity to decide who should look after their estate, their financial affairs and any investments. We could have stayed with the firm that the family had used before but, for me, there were issues around lack of engagement, the need for hands-on advice and an understanding of me and my needs; we just weren't that close professionally.

The age and health of their company was a real concern for me. It was summed up perfectly by a brilliant introduction at a networking event from an independent financial advisor, who said: 'If your financial advisor is the same age or older than you, come the time you wish to retire, they will probably already be retired or dead!'

This was exactly how I felt, so we looked elsewhere. Within a year of moving from this firm, the senior partner had triple heart bypass surgery and very nearly didn't make it through the procedure. This was, for me, a close call in my professional support team.

Choosing a new firm, moving everything over and starting anew is a daunting prospect. Can you trust them? Are they any good? How much due diligence should you be undertaking and what does that look like? Who has recommended them? What makes them unique when there are so many others out there? What will it cost? 'Test and measure' is a phrase referred to in many industries; the carpenter always measures twice before cutting, so you should measure and evaluate more than once before jumping in with your new team.

This new relationship is going to become long term; you are not going to jump around and change providers every year. You need to get to know them well because if they succeed in looking after you and your family, this could end up being a 50-year partnership. You need to invest the time. Choose someone with skin in the game who practises what they preach; test them along the way with small investments or projects to establish trust and confidence. When you start to see positive results, you'll give them more scope.

Various levels of risk are available in the world of wealth, from FCA-approved strategies to the rest of the market where the risks and rewards can be more significant. Be aware that the unregulated market is also the area where the sharks swim, so you will need to undertake far greater and detailed due diligence.

I have been hit directly by three massive market changes – in 2000, 2008 and 2020. In 2000, I worked for a start-up based in Perth, Western Australia. Three weeks before we were due to pitch for investment, a company in the same building won a seven-figure investment. By the time we pitched, all the money had gone. The game had changed in an instant, making the experience very painful. However, as a result, our business model changed and, six years later, the company was bought out by a national organisation.

After the banking crisis in 2008, millions were wiped off share portfolios and professional funds, property prices plummeted and government-funded business contracts disappeared. Global losses were huge, and so were my own. In all honesty, in 2008 I did not have proper wealth management in place and, looking back, my approach was borderline reckless. I had invested in areas that a wealth manager would have been unlikely to support. It was a valuable, and costly, lesson to learn.

The effects of the global pandemic in 2020 will take years to be fully understood. Some businesses have failed while others have been able to grow and innovate. With a long-term investment strategy in place, it will be easier to survive recessions and market corrections when they come.

Markets will always go up and down, so one basket is a dangerous place to put all your eggs. A wealth manager will focus on a balanced portfolio of investments to manage risk according to the investor's individual appetite for risk and financial requirements.

I am not a financial advisor, but I do work closely with several of them and have a firm that looks after my family's wealth. You need to invite and challenge your wealth manager and professional support team to give you the appropriate levels of support. I guarantee it will help you sleep better at night!

The legal eagle

Are there times when you don't think your business partners are playing the same game as you? Do you fear you could be left carrying the can if something goes wrong? Personal and professional deals can go sour. What could you do to make sure this doesn't happen?

Your solicitor's primary role is to provide objective legal advice in many different situations; they are your legal eagle and can spot a potential issue from afar. While no one enjoys spending money when they can't see an immediate need for it, having a solicitor on your team from the outset can prove worthwhile in the long run.

When the clock starts ticking on legal advice, it can be scary. However, at the beginning of a collaboration, creating a business 'prenup' is crucial and will save a lot of heartache at a later date if and when relationships break down or end. Not all couples think about getting a prenuptial agreement before making a lifelong commitment to each other, but if and when the proverbial hits the fan, many wish they had.

Not every situation needs a legal eagle looking over your shoulder, but for peace of mind it's good to have them ready and waiting in the wings. In business there's a pile of legal paperwork around every corner, and only the experts know what to look out for and how to extrapolate its true meaning. Just talking about legal eagles has made me use one of the longest words in the whole book!

In business, the terms and conditions (T&Cs) can help or hinder agreeing a deal and getting on with the work, but that slight delay can be well worth it to protect you and your business. Several years ago, I was in final rehearsals with a client company and their directors to deliver an extensive programme. The CEO decided to attend for the first time in the process, and there was a clash of ideas on how everything was to proceed. In a heartbeat, my contract was cancelled. Fortunately for me, they had signed my T&Cs, which included a watertight 100% cancellation fee.

Thankfully, the client was willing to fulfil the signed contract. I did agree to a negotiated fee, meaning I was paid a great deal of money to not deliver anything. It doesn't get much better than that with a cancellation. Fortunately my relationship with the client was undamaged and I have continued to work with them in other areas.

Legal advice might seem expensive and easy to avoid or ignore, but there are so many stories out there that demonstrate how vital taking that advice can turn out to be. Sadly, I have been on the other side of the fence, when I trusted the process and didn't want to incur additional costs. I ended up taking a regrettable shortcut some years ago when I bought an overseas property. I used the developers' solicitors rather than my own, and got royally screwed. It has cost me a great deal of money every year for far more years than I would like to admit. If only I'd sought independent legal advice.

I wasn't entirely naive; I did research a variety of property investment opportunities. What I failed to do, however, was thoroughly investigate the partners I was going to be working with to check that they had the necessary knowledge to achieve my goals. It hurt a great deal, and all because I didn't have a professional support network making sure I wasn't exposed to the sharks.

They say that wisdom comes from learning from your own mistakes. Yet by taking a step back, challenging those around us in a supported environment and accessing collective wisdom, these mistakes will be fewer and farther between. And when mistakes do happen, we will be able to ride the storm more effectively.

Legal support comes in so many different guises. There are generalists and specialist lawyers, one-person bands, small and large practices. Work out what you need and commit to paying for the advice.

Lawyers cover all sorts of areas:

- **obligations – contracts, employment, franchises, etc.**
- **ownership – buying or selling, conveyancing**
- **rules – terms and conditions, modus operandi**
- **conflict of interest – clashes, disputes, arguments**
- **malicious intent – fraud, criminal activities**
- **agreements/matrimonial – personal or professional, prenuptial or divorce**
- **human resources – hiring and firing.**

If you're moving house, hiring a solicitor to do your conveyancing is relatively straightforward. However, you may not currently know what your legal responsibilities are in a non-executive director role or the management buyout you are considering.

It takes just one phone call to ask someone on your professional support team for the appropriate connection. You trust them and know the probability of them introducing you to the best person is high.

Seeing through promotional propaganda is one of the objectives of your professional team.

We've all seen the 'make a million dollars in your sleep' adverts on social media where you just need to follow their simple formula to get rich quick, after you have paid a small fee. Recently I was talking with a woman who lived next door to someone who promoted one of these schemes. To impress their readers with demonstrations of material wealth and success, they took photographs of Ferraris and other sports cars. Sadly, the photographs were all stage managed and the vehicles were hired for the morning.

Is this unethical? You be the judge. Much motivational advice follows the mantra 'fake it till you make it'. While that whole approach might not cross any legal boundaries, it does not sit well within my own moral code and makes me question what reputation they are trying to build.

The morals of an individual or a company have a massive impact on their performance and professionalism. What is the intention behind the information you are receiving from a business, employer or developer? Are you the best person to investigate or uncover the hidden speed bumps ahead? If your gut feeling is 'not quite sure', then seek legal advice and be prepared to pay for it.

The accountant

There is so much more to your accountant than just making sure you are paying your taxes on time, and not a penny more than you need to. This is clearly one of their most important roles. But there is also a balance required between a compliance accountant and a management accountant. One talks to HMRC or the IRS and calculates how much tax you should pay; the other shows you whether you are currently making any money from what you are doing and where you either need to tighten your belt or put your prices up.

As with the legal eagle, the accountant is often referred to as a necessary evil. That doesn't mean they can't be fully involved and helpful, enabling us to find the best way forward from a strong financial foundation.

After the 2008 market collapse, not only did my wife and I change our wealth management team, we changed accountants as well. The decision wasn't made because we were getting poor advice, it was because we needed a more coordinated and involved approach to our finances going forward, which was not an option with the incumbent accountants. Yes, I sought advice and recommendations from other members of my support network and, after a considerable amount of time, the decision was made. Overall I would say the approach was very similar to changing our wealth management team.

'What gets measured, gets done' is a quote attributed to many people over the years. What are your sales figures, your gross profit, net profit, break even, hidden costs, marketing and advertising, salaries, PAYE, taxes, etc? Are there any specific areas where you are vulnerable because of missing information that currently masks future issues yet to be uncovered? A good accountant will give you real, honest and quantitative data that will enable you to make informed decisions when those significant events happen outside of your control. Do not under-use them because you're trying to pinch pennies; they could uncover gems and details that make all the difference in your business.

Accountants need details and numbers to help make decisions and provide sound financial advice. Choose the measurement tools that are appropriate for you, supported by your professional team. This will get you the accurate financial information needed to make long-term strategic decisions as well as urgent ones where necessary. Remember, you are in charge of your finances and make the decisions that enable everything to happen; you are only guided by your advisors.

Risk management often has negative associations, but planning for the unexpected is wise. What would happen if you were not capable of working, due to injury, illness or mental incapacity? How are you going to keep the financial wheels turning? Food still needs to be put on the table, and if you're not earning, how long can you last without burning through any or all your savings?

All potential investors and accountants carry out a simple risk analysis in the form of due diligence checks on any investment opportunity.

Look at your own business. Is it built on a solid foundation that you would want to invest in yourself?

Time to share some simple maths.

♟ **Step 1 – What do you need to take out of the business every month to pay for the lifestyle that you currently have?**

♟ **Step 2 – Now multiply that by 36 months – three years. Not overly challenging.**

If you were to invest in a business, would you invest the sum you have just calculated into your business? Most investors want their investment back within three years, plus a serious return on top. Is this achievable?

With the backing of accurate financial information and support from your accountant, your interests can grow and prosper. What are the golden rules of business and life that work for you? Write them down, stick them up in your office, share them with your family, friends and colleagues.

In sport, if it's still mathematically possible to win, you cannot quit. If you ease off the pace, switch off mentally or just go into cruise control, your coach will kick you. Think of the football match where the team is down by two goals going into injury time, and they come back to win; or the tennis player who is two sets and a break down and eventually triumphs.

Coming back from a negative position is something that sportspeople have prepared, planned and trained for with a team supporting them. Working blindly and hoping you can overcome a financial downturn without actually knowing your net profit or how much money you have in the bank can be fatal in business. In the world of finance nobody likes surprises; being in possession of the full facts will help prevent foolhardy optimism, misguided loyalties or bad decision-making.

A question of trust

Your professional support team only works if you have trusting relationships. When I consider the word trust, I immediately think of my children or money, i.e. who would I trust to look after my children if I died suddenly and to whom would I entrust the management of my money? For many, making this decision often comes down to a gut feeling. Emotionally charged, life-changing or tough decisions all become far less stressful when your professional team talk to each other about the best choices for you as a client. They can discuss future investments and relationships along with business and private exits, all of which will save you a lot of money in the long run. A team looking at all areas of your life will make a world of difference to your finances, peace of mind and wealth.

For me, trust means that I have confidence in or can depend on a person or a process. Without trust, you cannot do business and you cannot delegate with confidence. Without trust, your life and business would come to a grinding halt; at some point, you have to trust others.

Throughout my life, I have been guilty of being both too trusting of others and also of writing people off too early who have turned out to be supportive in the long run. When people appeared to have similar values and drivers to myself, I have often trusted them too quickly. It has been easy to discount others whose approach is different to my own. While gut instinct is important, a trusted advisor can add so much value and give you the back-up you might need to make that decision.

Reflecting on my adventures in overseas property investing, I really wanted the people I was working with to be the experts. Sadly, this caused me to confuse trust with the hunger to succeed, and this led me down the path of failing to do enough due diligence until it was too late. My desire to build an attractive property empire that would make me financially independent overrode my gut feeling and meant I chose to ignore the warning signs that in hindsight were clearly visible.

Being a naturally optimistic person, I tend to look for the good in people and assume they are genuine and know what they are doing. There are situations where my instinct tells me something doesn't quite add up, and I have now learned (the hard way) that how you respond to these internal alarm bells can save or make you a fortune.

Without trust, there is no relationship. Trust your instinct; it will be spot on most of the time. Build trust with the partners in your professional team. With solid legal, wealth management and accountancy support, your foundations for mental wealth will be underpinned, giving you peace of mind and a strong sense of security.

The professional support checklist

Building a professional support team will help you avoid unnecessary amateur mistakes. Where are you currently vulnerable or potentially exposed? Find the professionals that are relevant to you and remember: choosing not to take professional advice can be more costly in the long run. Here's how to choose well:

♟ Take advice from other members of your support team.

♟ Ask for introductions from those you respect.

♟ Don't be intimidated by stereotypes – these professionals are all human beings.

♟ Accept that you do not need to know all the answers – that's what your team is for.

♟ Accept that a good professional team costs money and the cost of getting it wrong is far greater.

♟ Create an environment where your professional team can talk to each other about the best way forward for you as a client.

♟ Trust takes time to develop – be patient and believe in the process.

♟ Follow your instincts – if you get a bad feeling, look for somebody else.

♟ When it's time for a better option, make a decision and move on.

The Mastermind Team

Masterminding can be the missing link that makes all the difference to your business and career. It's about creating an environment where you can meet compelling people who are looking out for you in the same way that you're looking out for them. But it's so much more than a professional sounding board; sometimes it can simply be about the seed of creativity that somebody else plants in the back of your mind.

Mastermind groups offer peer support and engagement, with the simple goal of helping each member succeed. They might be called different names by other organisations, such as peer coaching or action-learning sets, but the essence is the same. You can find mastermind groups of all kinds, from businessmen and women and professional speakers to teachers, book publishers and former or retiring professional sportspeople. Members meet to support, learn from and challenge each other, and discover the skills and ideas they would not get in their usual working environment.

A facilitator or chairperson runs the group and, in between meetings, members hold each other accountable for the actions they have committed to. As a member of a mastermind group, an individual commits to support other members fully while keeping complete confidentiality and respect for their fellows.

There are many different frameworks for mastermind groups. Just because it's set up in a certain way on day one doesn't mean that three or 18 months down the line the structure will still work for you. Make a change or join a different group; you need to find a good fit. You can even join multiple groups, each addressing a different aspect of your personal/business life.

If you're setting up a group and you have the optimum number of members involved, you'll have to agree on the number and style of the meetings. Be flexible – some people prefer to meet face to face, while others prefer Teams or Zoom. Make sure it works for everybody.

One of the most significant benefits of masterminding is accountability. There is no point in joining or setting up a mastermind group if you're not prepared to be held accountable or take action. At the end of a meeting you will hopefully be able to make a closing commitment that sounds a little like this: 'OK, my name is Mike. I'm going to do these three things before we next meet.'

What are the three things you're going to do as a result of your mastermind group meeting? Whatever they are, you need to take action, and at the same time hold your fellow members accountable to what they say they're going to do.

As always in life, problems will inevitably arise within a group. How do you deal with people who are talkers and take no action? What about those that take more than they give? The more potent the mastermind group environment that you create, the more likely it is to be successful, and those that don't fully commit will be left behind. And that's what you need; you want to feel it's worth giving up time, energy and effort to support the other people in the room. It works both ways. As a result, you'll be achieving more, as will they, making it a hugely worthwhile investment for all.

A short history of masterminding

Time for a brief history lesson. Masterminding has been around a long while; it has seen many guises with much debate over its origins.

The Americans claim Napoleon Hill was one of the instigators of masterminding through his book *Think and Grow Rich*, written in 1937. However, let's go back even further in time. What you'll find is that masterminding originates from an organisation called the Lunar Society, which was set up in Birmingham, in the West Midlands, back in the 1760s. Its original members were the luminaries, business leaders, engineers and intellectuals of their day, with founders including Matthew Boulton, Erasmus Darwin, James Watt and Josiah Wedgwood.

It is said that meetings were held when the moon was full so that members could travel by moonlight – hence the Lunar Society. They got together as a group to discuss and debate ideas for the future, some of which were very left field, creative and potentially going against the grain of societal and religious beliefs of that time.

We are talking about the dawn of the Industrial Revolution, when engineering and modernisation were happening at such a high pace that people were scared. Because of this, the Lunar Society met in secret. Why would these visionary men need such an environment to get together? The answer is simple – even visionaries don't know what to do sometimes!

It's tough at the top

These days, the feeling of isolation at the top can be immense. Sharing your fears with stakeholders or shareholders could reflect poorly on you within a company. Maybe you're the boss, so you're expected to know the answers. Telling co-directors you need help can leave a perception of incompetence and lack of knowledge and skills.

Your spouse or partner is a natural person to confide in, but they aren't necessarily the best person to give you strategic business advice. Your friends in the club, in the pub or on the sports team always say: 'Just go for it, Mike, you always land on your feet.' So who else can you talk to?

What about your employees? Let's be honest, it might not always be appropriate to tell them that you don't know all the answers. However, empowering them by getting them involved in the decision-making process can create many alternative options for you and get your staff more committed to the organisation. There are examples to be found across hundreds of business school textbooks where successes can be directly attributed to the empowerment of employees.

If you feel that you have nowhere else to go for confidential, impartial advice or just an alternative perspective, who or what are you left with? For many that leads to isolation. This is when being involved in a mastermind group can be advantageous. It is a safe space where everyone can be honest, direct and not worry about offending or upsetting anyone.

You don't have to be one of those visionary leaders from the late 18th century to benefit. The concept is just as relevant in the 21st century. Whatever you do, you need the support of your peers because building or running a business on your own is hard work. Give your mastermind group permission to challenge you and hold you accountable to your promises.

One of the things I have always found difficult is learning how to be truly honest and open when I don't have all the answers. I used to feel it was a sign of weakness. I'm well educated, I've taken extra qualifications, I read books, I have an IQ in double figures. But when I started masterminding, I still felt uncomfortable opening up and asking for help, letting people get into my head and challenge me. But once I did, I was able to really learn and develop. Joining or creating a mastermind group will help you open up and reduce the feeling of isolation as you discuss your ideas with like-minded people.

A clear example of isolation came from my father-in-law who, after reading my views on masterminding, shared these words:

> In looking back on my own experiences and particularly my darkest years of running a business I knew I was going to have to close, I can see how I might have benefited from some of the support systems you are advocating. I was responsible for building my own team and had plenty of support from that, but they were the last people I could be open with in discussing what I perceived to be the end result. Neither could I discuss it with my peer group [the board] because, with a single exception, they considered the closure of the company unthinkable. Indeed, they were very nearly proved right and we only escaped disaster by a whisker. Perhaps I might have benefited from a mastermind group, but between the emergency internal meetings and being summoned to instant meetings with the banks in London I doubt whether I would have been able to attend very often.

He was a successful businessman but now, at the age of 80+, has demonstrated how he, despite having a large team around him, became isolated during some of the most challenging times in his business. Fortunately, the working world has moved on and emergency meetings in London can be carried out online; but his story does reinforce how tough it can be at the top. Having the support of a mastermind group can make a massive difference.

The rules of engagement

You need to experience vulnerability without feeling threatened, so be prepared to let down your guard and accept feedback that is honest, direct and sometimes personal. To achieve this goal, there are a few critical rules of engagement.

Rule 1: Confidentiality

Masterminding only works if the foundation stone of confidentiality is in place. I've run many mastermind groups where, as a condition of joining the group, everyone signs a confidentiality contract. It's a one-page agreement to commit to the rules of the group. Simple as that. Whether or not it would stand up in a court of law is not the issue here. The point is to make sure that the overall agreement is: 'I respect the rules of this environment and I am going to work within them.'

This rule stems from the Royal Institute of International Affairs at Chatham House, as quoted here, written in 1927:

When a meeting is held under the Chatham House Rule, participants are free to use the information received. But the identity or the affiliation of the speaker or speakers, and all that of any other participants may not be revealed.

This means you can have heated debates and discussions, but nothing leaves the room with a name attached to it. So you won't have to worry that anyone is going to start telling your competitors you've got problems with your supply chain, you're not comfortable with some area of your life or you have concerns about various staff members. It even stretches to knowing that nobody will tell others about the illness you've just revealed to fellow members and isn't yet public knowledge.

In today's digital world, where everyone has a camera or a voice recorder, privacy and confidentiality are essential. The Chatham House Rule means that boundaries are set correctly from the start, and is the way all professionally run mastermind groups work. If you're considering joining a group and they are not focused on confidentiality, I wouldn't join.

Rule 2: Set objectives for the group

You can set up a mastermind group to make your business more productive, achieve a sporting challenge, write a book or learn a new language. I know a mastermind group where all members are professional speakers. They spend all their time challenging each other's content and delivery style and how their business works, while supporting each other mentally, emotionally and practically.

By contrast, many business mastermind groups are made up entirely of organisations that aren't in competition. Members' companies are often so diverse that, to begin with, there is little or no exchange of insider knowledge. One question that always goes down well when starting a group like this is: 'How does that work in the real world, because I can't see how you can make money?'

When the aim is clear to everybody, it becomes far easier to avoid groupthink and non-productive chitchat, meaning you're able to get focused on that purpose in everything you do. The more specific the goal, the easier it is to measure the value of membership for all in attendance.

Rule 3: Set the structure and environment

If you're setting up a framework where, say, everybody gets 10 minutes or an hour-and-a-half to talk, then you must enforce that rule. Whether you're self-managing or have an appointed chairperson, you need to stop people waffling. There is always someone who, if they are allowed to, will use up twice the amount of time allocated, meaning others later in the agreed order run out of time, which can cause resentment and frustration.

Choose a physical environment where you're able to discuss, debate, be open, vulnerable, honest, scared and real. Is your house suitable or not? Do you need a conference room, a hotel or somewhere that is neutral territory for all?

Take the location seriously. Masterminding is not something you can go into light-heartedly; it demands focus, direction and clarity of vision. Identify what you want to get out of it as a result. It is not a visit to the pub, or sitting down with a few mates over a couple of glasses of wine while debating world events. It's all about action and accountability, which requires a clear structure and the right environment.

Rule 4: Numbers

How many members constitute a mastermind group? I believe five to seven people is the optimum number, because not everyone's always going to be available. You want to have a minimum of five people in the room, five people who can debate and question. The fact that a member is not here this month or this week is not a problem, because somebody else will ask questions and the absent member will ask his or her questions the next time.

By contrast, in a large group, someone's voice may not be heard and it is difficult to develop a good debate. The larger group will eventually break into smaller groups anyway. The challenge is to make the event formal enough that members respect the process but it is not so structured that it becomes overbearing or bureaucratic. Masterminding needs that natural flow and evolution which comes from a smaller group.

Rule 5: The chairperson

When you are a paid-up member of a mastermind group, the chairperson is likely to be the instigator and facilitator of the group meetings. However, if you run your own meetings the role of the chairperson may change.

As in all meetings, the chairperson's objectives include managing the energy in the room as it ebbs and flows throughout the session. Quite often, groups will rotate the chair, meaning they have a different facilitator who manages the clock or the discussion at each meeting. I would advocate this as it prevents the outspoken people from controlling the group.

The chairperson needs to consider their management strategy depending on how different members operate. They are there to bring the best out of all members, manage the domineering personalities and make sure the quiet ones get their voice heard. They also instigate the breaks. I can only sit down in one place for a limited amount of time before I have to get up and move about. The chair will need to take this into account so that the group can work optimally.

If things get a bit heavy, the chairperson will need to call a time out. With a respected chairperson who demonstrates the necessary command, the group becomes far more powerful.

Rule 6: Honesty and feedback

Giving and receiving feedback is a skill that many people have to develop because it doesn't come naturally to everyone. Interpreting what is shared by the group in a positive mindset can be a challenge when your first instinct is to react defensively and take it personally. As you get to know the members of your group, feedback may become more direct, with the delivery style adapted to fit each member. That kind of feedback can be painful to hear and does risk getting people's backs up at times, but often that's what's needed to shake people out of their complacency.

Rule 7: Give and take

Regularly review everyone's commitment to the group and its rules. Is anyone good at talking but not so good at supporting? Just because people are enjoying the meetings doesn't mean the current set-up is effective. If a member is giving the process lip service, then the chances are they're not going to be pushing themselves forward. That leads to the big question: are they right for the group? If the answer is no, you must have the difficult conversation to encourage them to step up or step away from the group.

Rule 8: Understanding outside influences

When someone appears to be underachieving, you need to ask them what else is going on in their life. The closer the group, the more insightful members become. Outside influences at home or issues with health or family will impact the performance of an individual member and potentially the whole group. A responsibility of the group is to help members to seek additional support when necessary.

Rule 9: Recognise when to call it a day

Members do leave mastermind groups, and new people join. Some people don't get what they were expecting or hoped for. It might be because they're not putting the required amount of effort in or not giving enough to other members. Or it might be that the other members of the group aren't right for them. The wonderful words of Zig Ziglar are particularly relevant here: 'You can have everything in life you want, if you will just help enough other people get what they want.' The dynamic within the group needs to be bang on so that all can benefit.

All groups will have a shelf life. I've been in a group where, after about 18 months, we became a group of friends, and ended up being too nice to each other. That wasn't what we signed up for; it wasn't delivering the agreed objective. Did we need to finish this mastermind, kill it entirely and set up a new one? In this case, there were several members ready to move on, and those remaining brought in new members. In effect, we started again with a small number of the original group. Bringing in fresh blood can reinvigorate a group so it starts working effectively again.

Rule 10: Accountability

This rule almost needs a chapter of its own. When you are working in isolation with minimal support, it is very easy to make ill-conceived or random promises to yourself. I'm not saying that you are a procrastinator: it's human nature to do the stuff you like first and avoid the things you don't like, especially if it feels a little uncomfortable.

The keyword here is permission. When you were a child, you always had to ask for permission. Have you grown out of it, or is it still there in the back of your mind? The mastermind group changes that. Once you have debated a topic, you have permission from the other people in the room to go for it. Then the only thing stopping you from doing so is you. Being held accountable means that, at the next meeting, you will turn up having done everything you promised to do. There can be no debate.

The world conspires against you from time to time, and a plan might have to change. I've been to meetings where only two of the three actions I'd committed to had been completed. Strictly speaking, I could have been thrown out of the group, but I'd completed four other actions, invalidating one of the earlier three actions.

It's all about making sure that you are going to deliver as promised. This inbuilt respect for the process helps to commit members to the format.

You cannot hide your failures within the mastermind group environment. The procrastinator's motto, 'If at first you don't succeed, deny you were ever trying', doesn't work here. Share your successes as well as your failures. Be open and honest about the things that haven't worked so the group can deconstruct and help you understand why. Was it the wrong action, the wrong timing, or were the wrong people involved? A post-mortem is so important for ongoing learning and to make sure that people stay with the group and see the fruits of their labours.

Not every step you commit to will be successful. By committing to three actions per month at ten meetings a year, you're held accountable for the delivery of 30 key actions to enhance your personal and professional success.

It's easy to focus solely on the person receiving the challenge. As a mastermind member, your responsibility is to the other members, putting them on the spot when they start squirming and coming up with lame excuses. Your fellow members have also committed to 30 actions. In a monthly mastermind group with seven members, there will be 210 committed actions put into place over the year.

The knock-on effects of one wasted or incomplete action are impossible to calculate. It's hard to place a financial value on each successfully completed action; if you could I'm sure it would be worth a lot.

Accountability under the auspices of the Chatham House Rule results in successful masterminding. If you're working in confidence, you can open up and trust in the support and honesty you'll receive; and accountability means you're going to deliver on your actions.

Choosing the right members

A mastermind group is only as good as its members. So, whether you're joining another organisation, a group that's already established, or setting up your own from scratch, it is important to consider the people in the group.

Focus on people that inspire you, that you want to be associated with, that encourage you, lift you up, excite you, get you stimulated and thinking imaginatively. The objective is creating a climate of mutual success. There's nothing better than sitting in a meeting listening to people at your table turn to you and say any one of the following: 'I've achieved X as a result of your advice... As a result of collective wisdom we're overachieving by 25% this quarter... We debated numerous options, and as a result of the support from this group, we built a palace.'

A famous masterminding success story tells how a member was preparing to sell his business. He had a price in mind, which he shared in confidence with his group. Everybody said he was wrong. 'Don't do it at that price; it's way too cheap. Let's come up with a better price.' As a group, they worked together to come up with a more realistic price that was going to be both achievable *and* outstrip the member's initial expectations.

The collective wisdom of the group put an additional £20m on the price, and he got it! None of the members earned a penny from the transaction; none of them were shareholders, meaning there was no vested interest for any of them. Of course, they have been looked after personally as a result of the sale, even though they had no part in the business itself.

In the first group that I put together, I invited six people to the opening meeting. We'd done a bit of a pre-vetting, which involved introducing ourselves to each other, saying what we were trying to achieve, what our business was, why we might fit into this mastermind group and what we would bring to the table. We also identified our challenges. All of this was summarised in a one-page document – a tangible item that demonstrated we were serious about getting involved.

At that point, there was a lot of inside information on every applicant, including websites, online profiles and very personal stories. Everyone turned up to the initial meeting but two didn't sign up as they felt the chemistry of the group wasn't right for them. There are all sorts of reasons why people choose not to join. The good news was that, at the end of the first meeting, these two said: 'Guys, thank you very much for your time. It's not for me, and I won't be committing.' And that's what you are after – people who are honest enough to step away and people who are willing to commit.

Ask direct questions of potential members about their mission, vision and direction. What are your three most significant challenges? Where do you need the most help now? If people aren't happy to share that information, then they're always going to be a bit standoffish. To make masterminding work, you must have that commitment.

With this first group, I was creative in how I invited people to join me. There were three people that I respected – I liked their business style and their energy. I asked them each to invite one additional person. This took it away from being just my group, so I wasn't the person that linked everyone. I wanted more diversity than just my team.

When you investigate the different personality styles that are out there, it's easy to see how some people will fit, and others are best left alone. If you have a room full of people with one particular personality trait, one of two things can happen. If they're all strong personality types such as tough battlers (to quote Charles Handy), then the chances are you're going to have very short meetings, and there won't be much debate because they don't want to go into detail. Whereas if all the members are detail oriented, then they're not necessarily going to be interested in how people feel; they just want to see an Excel spreadsheet. The meetings may be long, drawn-out sessions with minimal decisions made.

The magic flows when members challenge each other's thoughts and beliefs; the more diverse the group, the more interesting it can become. One particular man I've worked with in a mastermind group was often taciturn during a meeting and did not appear fully engaged. However, he would come out with these pearls of wisdom, almost like dropping a 'mic bomb'. It was amazing to observe; on occasions, whole conversations changed, along with the entire structure of the challenge being considered at the time. So even though he didn't always speak, he brought massive value. You don't need people being talkative for the sake of it. He was very insightful and came up with some beautiful left-field suggestions.

Be aware of potential clashes in advance. In a business mastermind group, you don't want people that are in direct competition with each other. When it comes to sharing, they will feel less inclined to be honest and open. However, complementary industries can work exceptionally well.

Don't be afraid of variety; it can add different perspectives that you wouldn't even have considered. I'm not just talking about colour, creed, age and gender. I'm also talking about industry backgrounds, local government or the third sector. The more diverse the group, the more creative the solutions.

The mastermind meeting framework

You've got the structure and the rules of engagement; now comes the big question: what framework is going to work for you and your members? I've broken these into simple elements: monthly, weekly or the retreat.

The monthly meeting

In my first mastermind group, the six of us scheduled monthly meetings for ten months of the year – no meeting in August and no formal meeting at Christmas, so we could go out and be sociable. Each session lasted a whole day. The reason for that was simple. It meant that every single member of the group had an hour-and-a-half allocated to them, in three segments.

This is how the monthly mastermind works. In the initial 15 minutes, the member shares what he or she has been up to, what activities, successes, achievements, progress made, and a general update on what's going on. Then there's a whole hour to focus on that member's challenges, opportunities and inspiration. Preparation is essential. There could be dozens of concerns or just three that you would like to investigate – the more specific, the better. During this time, the rest of the members are in listening mode only.

The members then go into digging mode, asking classic, open 'what, where, when, why, how' questions, designed to get to the truth of the situation. They're not providing solutions, answers or suggestions; it's all about getting more insight into the particular issue. The objective is to get under the skin of the situation and uncover all the barriers and challenges.

Preventing people from going into fix-it mode can be a real challenge as the solution can often appear obvious to an outsider with zero emotional connection to the issue. Sometimes you will have to stop a member from speaking. I have had to call out 'zip it' (with a smile on my face) to one individual who just couldn't stop themself throwing in solutions too early in the process.

It's usually obvious when all investigation has been exhausted. Only at that point can solutions and options be shared and debated. There is still a need to manage this process, as you would in a coaching relationship. If you tell people what to do, they are far less likely to see it through than if they discover it for themselves with your help.

Then there are 15 minutes to hear conclusions from each member, creating multiple options to choose from. The person who's been challenged will then turn to the group and say: 'Thank you for all the input. Here are the three actions that I commit to completing before our next meeting.'

The question must then be asked: 'Can you honestly do that before we meet next month?' Don't say you will if you can't. Every meeting is scheduled, e.g. the second Tuesday of the month, so you know how long you have before the next meeting.

I confess that, on numerous Monday nights before a meeting, I've been found burning the midnight oil, finishing everything I had committed to completing. If that's what you need to do to complete your commitments, then do it – the momentum will follow. You must respect others' advice and support. Why would anyone want to give you their pearls of wisdom, their brain time, if you're not going to do anything with it? There is no excuse for not following through on your pledges.

In addition to the meetings, you will have access to continued support from your fellow members and buddy partners by phone or email. Not using this valuable resource between sessions makes no sense at all. You should be buddying up with different people and potentially collaborating on various projects.

Six people meeting together every month throughout the year equates to 50 days a year of external, impartial consulting added to your business. There is no time off in a mastermind day whether you are in the hotseat or asking the questions, you are constantly engaged, learning and debating opportunities, scenarios and alternative options – there is no rest here! How expensive would it be to buy that level of external input on the open market? That is why masterminding is so valuable.

Sitting on the other side of the table and asking the questions is just as powerful. It's not just about being on the receiving end, because in that one day you are consulting, coaching and cajoling the others.

At the end of a mastermind day, you will be tired. Your brain has been working non-stop as you challenged everyone else in the room, in the same way they challenged you. One of the greatest insights into my own world of procrastination has been when I've been busy grilling a group member and realised I hadn't been taking any of those actions myself. It can be very uncomfortable. You learn so much about yourself, as well as others, around the table.

I find the monthly mastermind framework is the way that most masterminds are set up – ten months of the year, something that is relatively straightforward to commit to. You do need to be careful as the group moves along, though, because people and businesses change and relationships evolve. What can often happen over time is that instead of it being a full day, the timings get pushed to half a day and perhaps the start time is moved to lunchtime with a presumption of going on into the evening.

Gradually, instead of it being a full day of an hour-and-a-half each, the time gets squashed, and you end up going out for a friendly dinner. All of a sudden, you only have three-and-a-half hours of actual work time divided by seven, which means the potency level is lost. Because of this, you lose out on the energy and momentum as you just become friends going out for a meal. You are left with the choice to either attempt to revitalise the group or just call it a day and join other mastermind groups.

I believe monthly meetings provide the best framework for long-term support and accountability; it's what the chief executive groups do.

Here's a simple summary of the monthly meeting framework:

- **every month except August and December**
- **actual time commitment: full day**
- **each member's time allocation: 1.5 hours**
    - 15 minutes: update on successes, progress and challenges
    - 60 minutes: challenges, opportunities, areas for debate and insights
    - 10 minutes: members' conclusions ('If I were running your business, I would...)
    - 5 minutes: conclusion, three commitments for next time
- **comfort break: next person**
- **in-between meetings – buddy support: ad-hoc phone calls, emails or face-to-face.**

The weekly meeting

Weekly mastermind groups work slightly differently to the monthly ones. They can turn into what some people might call scrum-downs in rugby, when everyone gets together for a short, sharp meeting to restart the game. In a mastermind format, they can last for anything between half an hour and two hours every week. The time of day and day of the week will vary for all, be that kicking off the week on a Monday morning or on a Friday afternoon at four o'clock to close the week. Every group is different. You choose.

The same criteria for selection and structure apply to the weekly framework. But, because of the frequency, you achieve a great deal of momentum. So, instead of choosing three or four actions at the end of a session, the member will choose one thing to work on. If you have six members, each person is only going to have 15 minutes maximum. The time is constrained for face-to-face meetings like this, creating a unique challenge that also presupposes you're all living locally to each other or work in the same environment.

A key question here: is it to be face to face or virtual? You can use whichever platform suits you – Skype, FaceTime, Zoom or Teams. The rules of engagement shouldn't change for virtual meetings; respect, punctuality, accountability, etc. are all the same whether or not you are physically in the room. There are some great clips available online showing the pros and cons of virtual meeting management; do your preparation so your meetings are fit for purpose. People used to be nervous about virtual meetings, but 2020 changed that.

In the virtual space, you have to be extremely well disciplined about structure and timings. One person running over means there won't be time to hear from some of the other members. Focused meetings with clear outcomes are a must. When it's this regular, people are going to leave at 9.30am precisely because they have appointments to attend.

As always, actions take place between meetings. If you're building on a particular area and want some collaborative help, assistance is easily accessible. You can arrange formal meetings or informal catch-ups online. By investing time into understanding what makes the other person tick, you can discover how you can be of real benefit to each other.

I've found that weekly mastermind groups have a shorter shelf life; they typically last months rather than years. They are great in giving you an intensive boost to kick-start a project or team. For this framework to be effective, you need to have very clear objectives for all members. Your membership will need to evolve with different people relevant for the next objective. By bringing in other people, you can get fresh inspiration and make the framework operate over an extended period.

I came across a similar format when I worked in the hotel industry, where we used to have a thing called morning prayers. It wasn't an actual prayer session, but we met at 8am for 20 minutes every day. The meeting was focused on what had been going on in the previous 24 hours and what was on the agenda for the next. Was it masterminding or just a daily catch-up? Whichever it was, there were definitely occasions where specific opportunities and challenges were investigated and resolved with peer support.

The weakness with the weekly mastermind framework is the lack of time at each meeting to dig deeply into fully understanding everyone's challenges. You can only deal with one thing at a time and work on that through to completion.

Summary of weekly meeting format:

- generally shorter project lead time
- actual weekly time commitment: 20 minutes to two hours maximum
- each member time allocation: 15 minutes
- update: one challenge, member insights, one commitment
- buddies, accountability and project partners in between sessions.

The retreat

I was taught about the retreat framework by a speaker friend of mine called W. Mitchell, from Colorado. Mitchell ran an international speakers' mastermind group, and instead of meeting monthly or weekly, they met three times a year when they happened to be in the same country at the same time. They came together for two days of intense challenge, provocation and accountability. All members got fully involved, sharing where their businesses were going, how they were working, and what help they needed to get to the next level.

The retreat can work exceptionally well if you have geographical challenges or time constraints. Rather than committing to a full day's meeting every month, meeting from Sunday to Monday every four months can often work better.

In the monthly framework, you have an hour-and-a-half allocated to each person. However, on a two-day retreat of six people, with the focus on three people each day, each member receives three hours of attention, or even more. That is why it can become very intense. Members can dig deeper, get more creative and investigate some of those more left-field ideas. They could pause to get some data and research, potentially evolving into a small project team that's working on a design or a launch for a member.

Even though there are lots of ideas in play, there is time to evaluate every aspect of the project and its feasibility. If members' businesses are complementary, as they were at Mitchell's speakers' retreat, then that kind of in-depth research can unlock even more value.

Once the retreat framework is created, the frequency can be adjusted to suit the members. It could be held twice a year or increased to four times a year.

A retreat takes you away physically, mentally and spiritually from your home, your office and your family. You will recall that I mentioned the positive effects of a training camp on elite sportspeople searching for that personal best or edge in their performance; the mastermind retreat has the same impact. You could duplicate this thinking for personal retreats that you might want to organise with a committed group of friends and participants.

An additional bonus of the retreat is the opportunity to socialise. The closeness and constant interaction can create powerful bonds. Follow-up phone calls and emails are critical, keeping up to date with what's happening with everyone, sharing successes and asking for further support when necessary.

Summary of the retreat format – three times a year:

- **each meeting takes two days**
- **actual time commitment: two days plus travel and overnight accommodation**
- **each member's time allocation – three to four hours:**
    - 15 minutes: update on successes, progress and challenges
    - up to 90 minutes: challenges, opportunities, areas for debate and insights
    - 30 minutes: market research, challenge
    - 45 minutes: evaluation and investigation by all members
    - 15 minutes: conclusion – three commitments for next time
- **buddy partners available as always via phone, email and social media.**

Why not consider a hybrid mastermind group? You start with one framework, be that monthly, weekly or a retreat; and then you adapt it. You might decide, for example, in the monthly version, that you're going to have a bonus retreat in January every year. By contrast, you can have a retreat at the end of year to evaluate what has been accomplished and plan for the year ahead. Also, at any point in time, a plan can be put in place to include a six-week project of weekly meetings as you evaluate specific projects before a potential launch. Hybrids offer further scope for you to gain even more from your masterminding.

The mastermind checklist

Masterminding helps you stay connected, inspires creativity, challenges your work and is therefore a vital part of your mental wealth approach. It can be thought of as a brainstorming session, but it's so much more potent than that. Here's why.

Going deep: Masterminding allows members to share what they would do if they were in your shoes. 'If I were running your business, Mike, I would do this, this and this, so why aren't you?' 'If I was involved in your organisation, Claire, these are the ways I would be looking at your strategy, and I would be considering these angles. Is there something missing that we haven't discovered yet?' If you have six people putting on their directors' hats, looking at you and what you're doing, what might they see? It makes a big difference.

Contacts: As soon as you join a group, you unlock a vast network that you probably didn't know existed. Even if you're connected to 1,000 or 5,000 people through your client relationship management (CRM) software or social media, your network will grow exponentially. These new contacts have different experiences or skill sets. They might have built businesses in Europe, Asia and America – and now you can get to know them.

Different filters: Others are looking at your problem or opportunity through their filters and conditioning, and they will see it differently. One question that you hadn't even thought of can sow a seed in the back of your mind that could transform your life and business.

Potential for collaboration: There are so many ways in which you can uncover opportunities and chances for collaboration with other members of your group. You never know when your skill set might add value – all because you are in an open and intimate environment.

Freedom to make decisions: A mastermind group helps you release the fear of failure. You are supported by people who help you to come up with solutions and ideas. Some suggestions might not work, and some might make you a multi-millionaire. That's the point – it's all about finding out which solutions work for you.

Mentoring support: You'll have the support of business veterans who've been there, done that. It's this kind of knowledge and experience that can have a massive impact on you and your business. Mentors like this will give you the confidence to take the brave direction.

The compound effect: Masterminding is a repetitive process. You have to build trust with the other members, and that takes time. Trust develops through the compound effect of regular meetings.

Buddy partners: You can further develop trust and understanding with your buddies through phone calls, emails and brief conversations between meetings. What happens over time is that members become very close confidantes. One of them might even be the best man or a maid of honour at your wedding or participate in some other significant event. There are so many ways in which these relationships can build and develop.

Prevention of hypocrisy: Do you feel like a hypocrite asking other people questions when you don't know the answers for your own business? It's so easy when you're observing from the outside. The great takeaway is that you can start focusing on potential solutions for yourself as a result of another member's time in the spotlight.

Time to set up your group. What's stopping you from choosing three other people who can invite one other person, and setting up your first mastermind group? Create your own rules of engagement and set the objectives to make this work powerfully for you.

If you get this right, you can move from mediocre to higher levels of success. You'll have access to a group of people that you can work with for many years as well as friendships for life. Some of my best friends are people I've been in mastermind groups with over the past 15 or 20 years.

Be selfish when putting together your structure and framework. After all, you're going to invest the time, energy and effort to make it happen. Remember, if it goes off the boil, turn up the heat, turn up the accountability, turn up the pressure. If that doesn't work, change the framework, get people out and get new people in.

The Mental Wealth Team Summary

Your mental wealth team comprises four foundational elements: you and your self-care, your coach, your professional support team and masterminding. With these four working together, your world will be in safer hands.

Throughout this book I have highlighted how isolation kills creativity and prevents decision-making. As the saying goes, 'No man is an island'; we are designed to work and be with others. Your mental wealth team will prepare you and support you through any challenges you are faced with.

Everything comes down to taking small steps that cumulatively make a massive difference in your mindset and sense of wellbeing. With the correct people supporting you, your journey becomes less of a roller coaster ride.

Each section of the book will probably have resonated with you differently, according to your current circumstances. As time goes by, another area might need more of your attention. Here's a quick recap on the key points.

Self-care is about consciously and intentionally keeping your mental and physical self in peak condition, most of the time. Your optimal self-care is built on whatever you do to look after yourself physically, emotionally, psychologically, nutritionally and spiritually. The starting point is to make yourself number one in your world; only when you are mentally and physically strong can you be of service to others. Looking after yourself is not being selfish – it will help you perform at your best more of the time.

Coaching is about discovering and unlocking potential and success. As a result of coaching, you create a plan for the way forward and commit to taking the necessary action.

Professional support provides you with great advice and specialist insight into areas where you are not the expert. Errors here can have huge costs, both financially and emotionally. The three broad subdivisions of your professional support are: wealth management, legal and accountancy. Why would anyone choose to take unnecessary risks by not taking independent advice? Take it from someone who learnt the hard way.

Mastermind groups provide you with that inner sanctum of committed peers who are there to help you personally and professionally. Their advice, questioning and left-field thinking will bring you creativity, accountability and direction. With a group of people helping you take the correct actions, you will make the necessary progress to achieve those big, hairy goals.

Ultimately everything comes down to choices; it's your choice what you do, which direction you head in and where you seek out support. Remember that not taking action to improve or change your situation is a choice to accept the status quo and remain where you are. You need to allocate time, energy and budget to building the mental wealth team that works for you. Do this with the help of those who are already part of your support network, enabling you to grow your mental wealth team quickly and effectively.

The Mental Wealth Team Scorecard

Where are you going to find people to join your mental wealth team? Think about who already fits the bill in your existing network.

The following scorecard (overleaf) is designed to establish an initial baseline score, highlighting the level of committed support you currently enjoy. There are no right or wrong answers.

Complete the following by scoring each person's commitment level to you from 1–10, where 1 is a low score, and 10 is a high score; then put your response in the commitment score column. Do not overthink these numbers; it's just down to how you feel about their level of commitment and support. The mental wealth team score calculation will be explained afterwards.

Add in the people that are relevant to you. Here are a few ideas to get you thinking:

- life partner
- husband
- wife
- parents
- children
- best mate
- doctor
- coffee shop owner
- neighbour
- school friend
- dentist
- pub landlord
- hairdresser
- bank manager
- life coach
- therapist
- sports teammates
- coach
- accountant
- solicitor
- wealth manager
- physio
- sibling
- mastermind team member

	Name	Commitment Score	Mental Wealth Team Score
1			
2			
3			
4			
5			
6			
7			
8			
9			
10			
11			
12			
13			
14			
15			
16			
17			
18			
19			
20			
21			
22			

	Name	Commitment Score	Mental Wealth Team Score
23			
24			
25			
26			
27			
28			
29			
30			
31			
32			
33			
34			
35			
36			
37			
38			
39			
40			
41			
42			
43			
44			
45			

Here is an interpretation of the scores. As you investigate the thinking behind the scores you initially gave, you might be tempted to change a count up or down. Don't fudge a score to fit into a category; your instinctive score is more often than not correct.

Score   **1–3**

These people probably know your name and may even say hello to you in the street, but it's very unlikely they would call you or you would call them. They are acquaintances at best, with no real connection and zero commitment to you.

Score   **4–5**

There's probably a specific reason why they know you. You could have met at the school gate, at work or on a sports team. If you broke down on the way to a match, they would come and pick you up; but if you weren't around for a few months they wouldn't worry or ask about your welfare. When that season or reason expires they might drift away. The relationship is at best only skin deep, as is their support for you.

Score   **6–7**

You know these people well, chat about things going on in your world and, on occasion, challenge each other over different views about politics and the state of the economy. They come from various settings and you meet up regularly or randomly. There is history developing here. Doing business with them or seeking out their professional input is not something you would ordinarily do, but they are good fun and you enjoy their company.

Score   **8–10**

These guys have your back. You've asked for their help and permitted them to be honest and direct with you. You are happy to be open, truthful and vulnerable with them because you know they won't judge you, even if they don't agree with you. They know intuitively when you have a problem because they check up on you. When you say you're going to do something, they hold you accountable; and if they disagree with your thinking or direction, they will call you out and challenge you accordingly. You can't hide from them as they are looking out for you and will say it as they see it. If they need help to convince you of something, they won't hesitate to liaise with other members of your 8–10 group.

Now is the time to make a record of these numbers. In the column marked Mental Wealth Team Score, put a tick in the box against all the names you gave a score of 8, 9 or 10, and add up those scores. For example, you may have two 8s, three 9s and a 10, making your score 53.

That number is your Mental Wealth Team Score, and will vary from zero to 100+. A low total or even a zero score is possible and provides a starting point that will help you focus on the gaps in your network, and your ability to ask for help and form sustainable relationships. Where do you need to ask for more support and commitment?

The higher the score, the stronger your mental wealth. You are likely to be in a reasonably stable place, surrounded by people you can trust and with whom you can be open and honest. I would expect a realistic number of people in your mental wealth team to be between 5-15. The reason the table has space for 45 names is to show the number of acquaintances you have that are not yet part of your committed team.

I've always quoted my late mother-in-law, who said that if you can count the number of best friends on more than one hand, they are not best friends. The question is: how committed are they to you? Please don't over-inflate your numbers just to boost your ego.

In time, your target score is over 100, which may or may not be realistic for you. At the time of writing, I am in a period of transition. Several people within my team are changing; some are less committed to me now than I need them to be, whereas a few new members are stepping up and adding real value. My current score is 74; it has been 100+ before and will be again.

How do family members fit on the scorecard? If they are part of your committed network, then clearly they can be included. However, there is a difference between blood loyalty and a genuine active team member. Be aware of two-way scoring here, where you might score them as a 9 and, if you were to ask them, they might only score you as a 5. What impact does that have on your relationship, if any? It shouldn't matter, because we are focused purely on building the team that supports you, not a symbiotic support group. Your skills and knowledge may not be relevant or necessary to them.

Complete this scorecard as often as you see fit. I'd suggest 90 days would be long enough to notice a difference. A key objective is to be able to reflect back on the strength of your mental wealth team during the good times and the bad.

Time to Get on with It!

Rules, fear, external pressure and lack of self-belief are just a few of the excuses we use for not taking action. I'm sure you're familiar with the phrase 'ask for forgiveness rather than wait for permission'. As a youngster, I did whatever I wanted, when I wanted. I never asked for permission and accepted the consequences when I broke the rules. By contrast, my best mate, who played all the same games and got up to the same antics as I did, seemed to get away with everything. The difference was that he had taken the time to learn the rules first before bending them to suit him. I learnt a lot from him, eventually.

I am reminded here of a very personal story. My wife and I were visiting the UK from Australia, where we were living and raising our young family. My mother-in-law had terminal cancer, and her health was deteriorating. When my wife suggested that we move back to the UK to be with her, my mother-in-law's response was: 'That means I have to hurry up and die so you can get on with your life. No!'

She was a fearless and wonderful woman who lived for another 18 months after that conversation. She allowed us to carry on living our lives the way we wanted to. I think of it as a selfless act of a very brave woman who helped us resolve a moral dilemma.

Far too often, I hear stories of individuals who don't take action until it's too late. Sadly, my father was one of those individuals whose pride and stubbornness stopped him from seeing a doctor for several years. He had cancer, and didn't survive it. Was that selfish of him? Yes, you could say that his lack of action caused an unnecessarily early departure, depriving his children of a parent and his grandchildren of an opportunity to learn from and enjoy time with their grandfather.

He sabotaged his very existence by not dealing with an important issue, because he came from a generation that didn't believe in inconveniencing others. Do not take this as a bitter rant against my father; I can't be angry with him because his attitude was down to his conditioning, his upbringing. But that doesn't mean it has to be the same way for me.

I hope you will be able to relate to each of these stories at some level. Seize the day or seize the moment. The question to you is: what are you avoiding dealing with right now? What decisions are you putting off? What are you waiting for before you take action? You don't need permission to move, to ask for help or see a doctor (if you need to). In your personal and business life, there will be areas where you are not the best person to fix something or to change the status quo. How are you going to deal with it? How are you going to make it work for the longer term? Time to stop holding back and get on with it.

The question I always ask of clients is: 'So what? What do you want me to think, do or believe as a result of what you are saying?' I ask myself that same question now as this book draws to a close. What do I want *you* to think, do or believe as a result of reading this book?

I want you to become number one in your world, to be top of your own agenda, to look after yourself first. Only when you are mentally and physically strong can you help others. I want you to ask for help more often and surround yourself with people who have your back. By asking better questions and with the support of others, your life will improve. You are going to make errors with or without a mental wealth team. The difference is that, with a mental wealth team, the errors are more likely to have been foreseen and the potential negative fallout can be managed effectively. Most importantly, you are not alone.

Whether you're an employee, an entrepreneur, a CEO, a student or a retired sportsperson, with a mental wealth team behind you, you will achieve more in life, discover the depth of your brilliance and leave a positive footprint on the world.

One of the outcomes from having a mental wealth team has been the writing of this book. I had written books before and lacked the desire to go through the process again. However, as a result of my discoveries, reflections, research and interviews, my business is changing and evolving. My approach and direction has been rewritten with a very clear target over the next five years, and I have already put the necessary support in place to help make those goals a reality.

Throughout your life your team will change and adapt; new people will join, and others will move on. When the wheels come off, like they did for my friend Tom, being able to rely on people who have your back can be a life-saver. Make the journey easier, more enjoyable and achieve higher levels of success by building the finest mental wealth team. Good luck!

Resources

Bart Dalton – 3G Advisor: bartdaltonconsulting.com

Charles Handy – tough battlers, friendly helps, logical thinkers: management study guide.com/charles-handy-model.htm

David Hyner, Stretch Development – Massive Goal Principle: stretch-development.com

Dr Edith Eger, The Choice – life-affirming strength and a truly remarkable resilience: dreditheger.com/the-choice

Eric Berne, Transactional Analysis: ericberne.com/transactional-analysis

Fred Reichheld, Net Promoter Score: netpromoter.com

Linda Ellis, The Dash: inspiredkindness.com

Dr Lynda Shaw, neuroscientist: drlyndashaw.com

Martin Goodyer, 80-year holiday: martingoodyer.com

Mike Pagan, The FAFFometer: stopfaffingabout.com

Richard Wilkins, Near Life Experience: theministryofinspiration. com/about

Robert Kaplan and David Norton, Balanced Scorecard: balancedscorecard2.com/history.html

Roger Harrop, the Man with the Helicopter: rogerharrop.com

Sarah Pagan, Good Companion: goodcompanion.uk

Shriya Joshi, Differences Between Being Alone and Being Lonely: storypick.com/lonely-vs-alone/

Stephen Sutton, Thumbs Up Stephen: facebook.com/StephensStory

Professor Steve Peters, The Chimp Paradox: chimpmanagement. com

The Karpman Drama Triangle: en.wikipedia.org/wiki/Karpman_drama_triangle

Victor Frankl, Man's Search for Meaning – lessons for spiritual survival: psychologytoday.com/us/blog/hide-and-seek/201205/mans-search-meaning

W. Mitchell, global masterminding – it's not what happens to you that matters, it's what you do about it: wmitchell.com

Useful UK & Ireland mental health support resources

Samaritans: free emotional support line, open 24/7, on 116 123, samaritans.org

Rethink Mental Illness: email advice@rethink.org or go to rethink.org

Sane: meeting the challenge of mental illness; emotional support, sane.org.uk

Beat: national charity for people with eating disorders, b-eat.co.uk

Mind: advice and support to empower anyone experiencing a mental health problem, mind.org.uk

Rethink Mental Illness: support and campaigning organisation for those affected by mental illness, rethink.org

Anxiety UK: support for those living with anxiety and anxiety-based depression by providing information, support and understanding, anxietyuk.org.uk

Minding Your Head: information on how to protect your mental and emotional wellbeing and the issues that can affect it, e.g. anxiety or depression, mindingyourhead.info

Self-Injury Support: charity that helps girls and women who self-harm, selfinjurysupport.org.uk

Support in Mind Scotland: support and empowerment for all those affected by mental illness, including family members, carers and supporters, supportinmindscotland.org.uk

Mental Health Wales: information for mental health professionals, clinicians, individuals living with mental illness, families and carers in Wales, mentalhealthwales.net

Hafal: mental health charity supporting those affected by serious mental illness in Wales, hafal.org

MindWise: leading Northern Ireland mental health charity working with those affected by and at risk of mental illness, mindwisenv.org

Aware NI: online support groups for people who are affected by depression or bipolar disorder in Northern Ireland, www.aware-ni.org

Turn2Me Ireland: offers free online counselling, chat and group support to promote good mental wellbeing, turn2me.org

Family and relationships

Gingerbread: expert advice and practical support for single mums and dads in England and Wales, gingerbread.org.uk

Working Families: help for working parents and carers and their employers to find a better balance between responsibilities at home and work, workingfamilies.org.uk

Family Lives: helping parents to deal with the changes that are a constant part of family life, familylives.org.uk

Working Mums: a centre of information for working parents with advice and support for people trying to juggle parenting and work, workingmums.co.uk

Home Start: support for parents as they learn to cope, improve their confidence and build better lives for their children, home-start.org.uk

Relate: relationship support for everyone, relate.org.uk

Family Therapy Ireland: the professional agency representing family therapy and therapists in Ireland, familytherapyireland.com

Alcohol and drugs

Al-Anon UK: support to anyone whose life is, or has been, affected by someone else's drinking, al-anonuk.org.uk

Alcoholics Anonymous: support related to the personal recovery and continued sobriety of alcoholics, alcoholics-anonymous.org.uk

Narcotics Anonymous: non-profit fellowship for recovering drug addicts, ukna.org

Action on Addiction: high-quality, effective residential rehab and community-based addiction treatment, actiononaddiction.org.uk

HSE Drugs and Alcohol Helpline (Ireland): hse.ie/eng/services/list/5/addiction/drugshivhelpline

Employment

Further education and skills: apprenticeship opportunities, apprenticeships.org.uk

Learndirect: UK's largest course provider, learndirect.com

National Numeracy Challenge: a free online tool to check your numeracy level, nnchallenge.org.uk

YESS Law: affordable legal advice to employees and employers who want to resolve problems at work, yesslaw.org.uk

Acknowledgements

First and foremost I'd like to thank my wife, Sarah, who is always the rock in my world. However, when it comes to writing, she becomes a grammatical, linguistic Rottweiler whose red 'track changes' feedback has been both brutal and blunt, highlighting the occasional error in my writing style and other peculiarities that don't work in print. I couldn't have done it without her.

And thanks to my children, who consistently remind me that I cannot guide or instil resilience in them and not follow through myself. Katie and Charlotte got hold of this book and trawled through page after page, challenging meanings that were not intergenerationally friendly, and helped uncover what I truly meant to say in particular sentences and paragraphs. And not forgetting James, adding support in the background, together with my father-in-law, who added his support and views from the other side of the generation gap.

To the current Mike Pagan mental wealth team – from finance and legal, coaching and fitness, to fun and travel – thanks to you all. We have surfed the waves of success and dug ourselves out of the various challenges that have presented themselves along the way. Without these guys supporting me, I would be making loads more mistakes or procrastinating in a dark room on my own. Thank you all for your ongoing support.

To the proofreaders in your masses: John Moody, Peters Richards, Francoise Brooks, John Owen, Ian Bluck, Nathan Gardiner, William Buist, Quentin Hayes, Marianne Goodson, Nick Owen, Philippe Ingels and last, but by no means least, Beverley Glick, who was given a task by the publishers to help unearth the diamond within the first manuscript and has overseen the creation of the book you're reading today. Thanks to you all.

Finally, thanks to Sue Richardson and her team at SRA Books for helping me become a genuine author. I have never thought of myself as a true writer or author, just someone who writes a few articles as part of my work and has published a couple of books before. I firmly believe this book will be my legacy.

About the Author

Mike Pagan is a superior executive coach with more than 25 years of combined corporate business management, coaching and consulting experience.

What makes Mike different? His approach is not standard – he can be blunt, direct, honest and open where necessary. All sessions are tailored and will reflect what is appropriate and needed by the coachee.

Mike is an expert in helping clients achieve positive mental wealth through strong support networks, unlocking significant performance improvements. His expertise includes working with entrepreneurial small businesses through to C-grade board members and partners in professional service firms, both UK and internationally.

Coaching: Mike's clients find their focus, become fully engaged and step into their potential. Not all coaches are right for you, your company or your team, so a two-way chemistry check is always necessary.

Process: Mike practises applied coaching, which always starts with a blank sheet of paper. The coachee dictates the direction of each session, their agenda and desired outcomes, according to simple rules of engagement.

Benefits: It is statistically proven that engaged employees are more likely to stay with an organisation, perform 20 per cent better than their colleagues, and act as advocates of the business.

Other professional development books published:

FAFF – The False Art of Feeling Fulfilled, 2010, 2nd edition 2012

The Business of Professional Speaking, collaboration, 2013

Is Your Business Fit For Purpose?, ebook, 2015.

To find out more, go to **mikepagan.com**